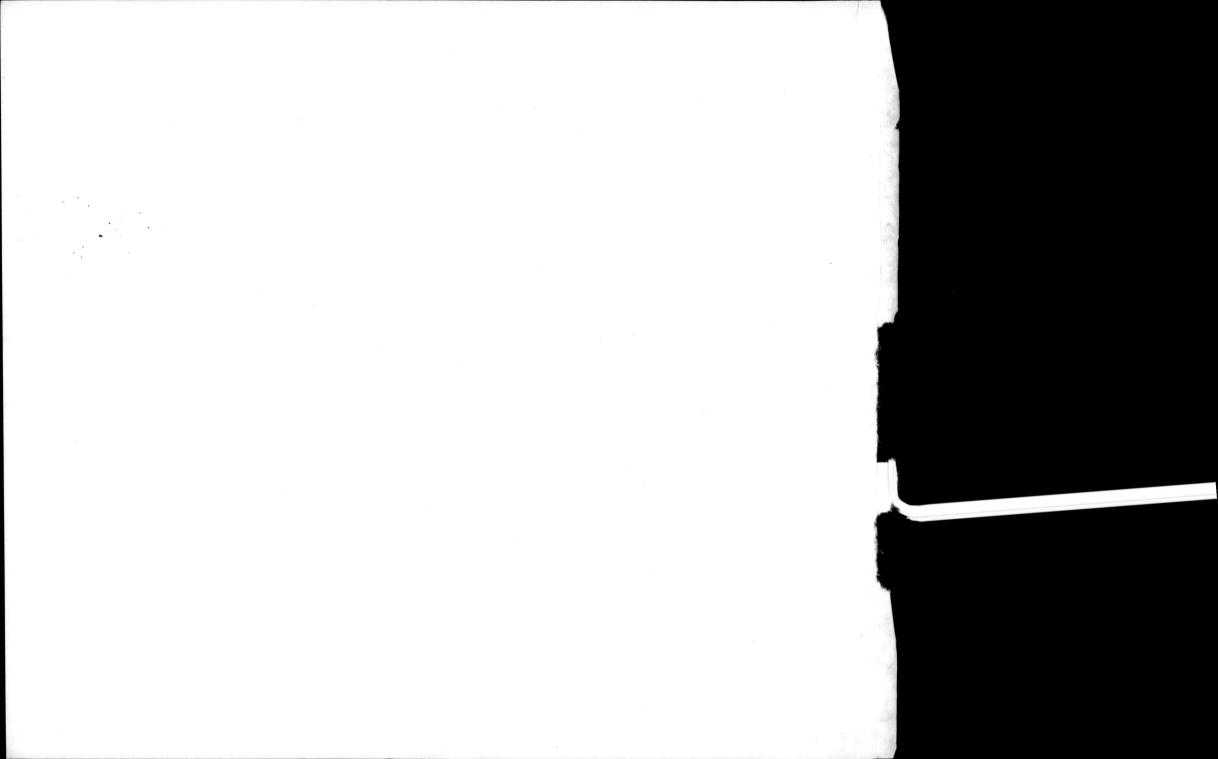

ELEMENTS, COMPOUNDS AND MIXTURES

⟨⊕⟩ Atlantic Europe Publishing

First published in 1998 by Atlantic Europe Publishing
Company Limited, Greys Court Farm, Greys Court,
Henley-on-Thames, Oxon, RG9 4PG, UK.

Author
Brian Knapp, BSc, PhD
Project consultant
*Keith B. Walshaw, MA, BSc, DPhil
(Head of Chemistry, Leighton Park School)*
Project Director
Duncan McCrae, BSc
Editor
Mary Sanders, BSc
Special photography
Ian Gledhill
Illustrations
The Ascenders Partnership, David Woodroffe
Electronic page make-up
The Ascenders Partnership
Designed and produced by
EARTHSCAPE EDITIONS
Print consultants
Chromo Litho Ltd
Reproduced in Malaysia by
Global Colour
Printed and bound in Italy by
L.E.G.O. SpA

Suggested cataloguing location
Knapp, Brian
    Elements, Compounds and Mixtures
    ISBN 1 869860 27 6
    – *ChemLab* series, volume 2
540

Picture credits
All photographs are from the **Earthscape
Editions** photolibrary except the
following:
(c=centre t=top b=bottom l=left r=right)
**Alcan International/British Alcan
Aluminium plc** 11bl, 11bc, 11br;
Mary Evans Picture Library 6cr, 7tr

Acknowledgements
The publishers would like to thank the
following for their kind help and advice:
**Alcan International/British Alcan
Aluminium plc**

*This product is manufactured from sustainable
managed forests. For every tree cut down at
least one more is planted.*

Contents

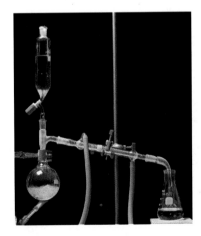

HOW TO USE THIS BOOK

These two pages show you how to get the most from this book.

❶ THE CONTENTS

Use the table of contents to see how this book is divided into themes. Each theme may have one or more demonstrations.

❷ THEMES

Each theme begins with a theory section on yellow-coloured paper. Major themes may contain several pages of theory for the demonstrations that are presented on the subsequent pages. They also contain biographies of scientists, whose work was important in the understanding of the theme.

❸ DEMONSTRATIONS

Demonstrations are at the heart of any chemistry study. However, many demonstrations cannot easily be shown to a whole class for health and safety reasons, because the demonstration requires a close-up view, because it is over too quickly, takes too long to complete, or because it requires special apparatus. The demonstrations shown here have been photographed especially to overcome these problems and give you a very close-up view of the key stages in each reaction.

The text, pictures and diagrams are closely connected. To get the best from the demonstration, look closely at each picture as soon as its reference occurs in the text.

Many of the pictures show enlarged views of parts of the demonstration to help you see exactly what is happening. Notice, too, that most pictures form part of a sequence. You will find that it pays to look at the picture sequence more than once, and always be careful to make sure you can see exactly what is described in any picture before you move on.

The main heading for a demonstration or a set of demonstrations.

An introduction expands on the heading, summarising the demonstration or group of demonstrations and their context in the theme.

Each demonstration is carefully explained and illustrated with photographs and, where necessary, with diagrams, tables and graphs. The illustrations referred to are numbered ①, ②, ③, etc.

Chemical equations are shown where appropriate (see the explanation of equations at the bottom of page 5).

The photographs show the key stages that you might see if you witness a demonstration at first-hand. Examine them very carefully against the text description.

APPARATUS

The demonstrations have been carefully conducted as representative examples of the main chemical processes. The apparatus used is standard, but other choices are possible and you may see different equipment in your laboratory, so make sure you understand the principles behind the apparatus selected. The key pieces of apparatus are defined in the glossary.

❹ GLOSSARY OF TECHNICAL TERMS

Words with which you may be unfamiliar are shown in small capitals where they first occur in the text. Use the glossary on pages 66–74 to find more information about these technical words. Over 400 items are presented alphabetically.

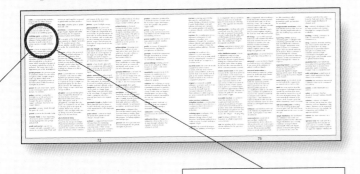

❺ INDEX TO ALL VOLUMES IN THE SET

To look for key words in any of the 12 volumes that make up the ChemLab set, use the Master Index on pages 75 to 80. The instructions on page 75 show you how to cross-reference between volumes.

The most important locations of the term 'oxidising agent' are given in a master index which includes references to all of the volumes in the ChemLab set.

oxidising agent: a substance that removes electrons from another substance being oxidised (and therefore is itself reduced) in a redox reaction. *Example:* chlorine (Cl_2).

ABBREVIATIONS

Units are in the international metric system. Some units of measurement are abbreviated, or shortened, as follows:

°C = degrees Celsius
km = kilometre
m = metre
cm = centimetre
mm = millimetre
sq m = square metre
g = gram
kg = kilogram
kJ = kilojoule
l = litre

❻ CHEMICAL EQUATIONS

Important or relevant chemical equations are shown in written and symbolic form together with additional information.

What the reaction equation illustrates

Where relevant, the oxidation state is shown as Roman numerals in brackets.

The symbol indicating the state of each substance is shown as follows:
(*s*) = solid
(*g*) = gaseous
(*l*) = liquid
(*aq*) = aqueous
(*conc*) = concentrated

Word equation

Symbol equation
The symbols for each element can be found in any Periodic Table.

EQUATION: Reaction of copper and nitric acid
Copper + nitric acid ⇨ *copper(II) nitrate + water + nitrogen dioxide*
$Cu(s) + 4HNO_3(conc)$ ⇨ $Cu(NO_3)_2(aq) + 2H_2O(l) + 2NO_2(g)$
Blue

The two halves of the chemical equation are separated by the arrow that shows the progression of the reaction. Each side of the equation must balance.

Sometimes additional descriptions are given below the symbol equation.

The correct number of atoms, ions and molecules and their proportions in any compound are shown by the numbers. A free electron is shown as an e^-.

ELEMENTS

An ELEMENT is a substance that cannot be broken down into simpler substances by any known means. Each of the 92 naturally occurring elements is therefore one of the fundamental materials from which everything in the Universe is made. Most elements are metals, but 22 are described as non-metals.

Elements are composed of ATOMS. A piece of sulphur is made entirely of sulphur atoms, and a lump of iron is made of iron atoms. When in a pure state, an element is described as elemental.

Elements can be combined in a reaction to form COMPOUNDS (see pages 8 to 17) or mixed to form MIXTURES (see pages 40 to 45). There are millions of possible compounds that can be formed.

Each element is represented by a symbol such as S for sulphur, Fe for iron, or Ca for calcium. Also, each element can be organised in order of increasing atomic number to make the PERIODIC TABLE.

Native elements

An element is described as 'native' if it occurs in the Earth's crust in an uncombined state as the element itself rather than as a compound. To exist in a native state, an element must be relatively unreactive.

There are about 18 NATIVE ELEMENTS, none of which is very common. Of the metals, native gold, silver, copper, tin and platinum are most commonly found and can be mined as ORES. They are normally found in underground seams called LODES.

Many native metals begin as hot liquids, which rise through the Earth's crust when volcanoes erupt. These hot fluids force their way up through the cracks in the overlying rocks, where they cool and solidify, depositing their solutes as CRYSTALS. Geologists call them HYDROTHERMAL DEPOSITS and prospectors call them ore VEINS. As well as gold, silver, copper, tin and

GREAT EXPERIMENTAL SCIENTISTS
Robert Boyle

Robert Boyle (1627–1691) who, along with Antoine Lavoisier, is considered to be one of the 'founding fathers' of chemistry, was born in Ireland, the 7th son of the 1st Earl of Cork. In 1654 he moved to Oxford, England, where he set up a small laboratory in his lodgings and later employed Robert Hooke as his assistant. Here Boyle invented the vacuum pump and, in 1622, he performed the experiments that allowed him to formulate a law relating pressure, temperature and volume of a gas, called Boyle's Law. In 1668, Boyle moved to London and became a well-known society figure. He was a friend of Sir Isaac Newton and Samuel Pepys. He lived in London until his death on December 30th, 1691.

Boyle experimented extensively on COMBUSTION and on the properties of acids and bases. He was the first scientist to separate chemistry from alchemy and to formulate a precise definition of a chemical element. He also distinguished between mixtures and compounds and demonstrated that compounds may have very different properties from their elements.

Boyle suggested the existence of simple atoms (which he called corpuscles) and that all phenomena could be explained in terms of the motion, shape, and position of these invisible corpuscles.

Boyle also invented the term 'analysis' and he introduced the plant extract, litmus, for testing acids and bases.

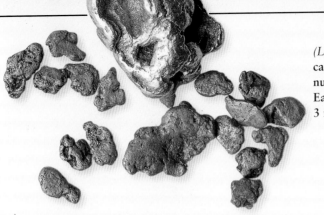

(Left) Native gold can be found as nuggets and flakes. Each flake is about 3 mm long.

platinum, the elements palladium, mercury, lead, iron, tantalum, zinc, arsenic, antimony, bismuth, tellurium and selenium each form native deposits.

Sulphur and carbon are the most common non-metals found in the native state. Sulphur is found as a common deposit close to volcanic vents where it forms mineable bodies called native sulphur deposits. Carbon is found as diamond and graphite, again usually associated with volcanoes.

Elemental gases

There are several elements that also occur naturally in an uncombined state as gases. They include nitrogen, which is the most abundant gas in the atmosphere, oxygen, and the unreactive NOBLE GASES such as argon and neon.

Sir Humphry Davy

Sir Humphry Davy (1778–1829) was a famous chemist born in Cornwall, England, who was the first to discover many metal elements, including sodium and potassium. He also proved that chlorine and iodine were elements. In later life he invented the miner's safety lamp.

Davy was trained as an apothecary and had to educate himself in science. Davy was fascinated by the ideas of the famous scientist, Antoine Laurent Lavoisier who worked with acids, bases and oxygen. Davy first began to experiment with light and heat. In 1801 he was asked to become lecturer on chemistry at the newly founded Royal Institution of Great Britain in London. In the following years, Davy made some remarkable discoveries and also was a very popular lecturer. One of those who saw his lectures was Michael Faraday, who was later made Davy's assistant before going on to become arguably the greatest experimental scientist of all time.

Just a year before Davy was made lecturer in chemistry, Alessandro Volta had made the world's first battery in Italy. He used it to dissociate water into oxygen and hydrogen, applying electricity to a process called ELECTROLYSIS. This exciting development determined the path of Davy's investigations and led, in 1808, to Davy isolating the metals sodium and potassium using electrolysis.

Davy also produced dinitrogen oxide (until recently called nitrous oxide) by heating ammonium nitrate. Years later it would be used as a dental anaesthetic (laughing gas). He designed the arc lamp for intense white lighting, produced a method for desalinating sea water and invented cathodic protection using contrasting metals on ships' hulls.

(Left) A piece of native copper on the surface of a mineral. The shape of this sample, which is about 10 cm long, is known as 'dendritic' and reflects the shape of the deep, underground, fissures in which it was originally deposited.

COMPOUNDS

A compound is a single substance made of two or more different elements joined together, or connected, by BONDS.

A compound has a fixed chemical composition. For example, the compound, water, always has twice as many hydrogen atoms in it as oxygen atoms (hence the formula for water is H_2O). Contrast this with a mixture (see page 40), which contains more than one substance, but which does not contain fixed proportions and so cannot be given a chemical formula. Unlike mixtures, the constituent elements in a compound are difficult to separate.

Also in contrast to mixtures, compounds do not inherit the properties of their elements. The properties of water (H_2O), for example, are quite unlike the properties of the elements, hydrogen and oxygen, from which water is made.

Also, when a compound is formed, energy is usually given out or absorbed (often as heat) whereas no energy change takes place in the formation of a mixture.

The fixed chemical composition of compounds also means that they have fixed physical properties, such as their boiling and melting points.

Bonding

The elements in a compound are held together by bonds that are either IONIC (①) or COVALENT (②).

① IONIC BONDS AND IONIC COMPOUNDS

(Below) Common salt, or sodium chloride (NaCl), is a common example of ionic bonding.

Both sodium and chlorine are very reactive elements. When they react, each sodium atom releases an ELECTRON, which is captured by a chlorine atom. The resulting sodium ions and chloride IONS are attracted to one another by strong electrostatic forces called ionic bonds to form the compound sodium chloride (see page 13).

As is typical of ionic compounds, sodium chloride has a high melting and boiling point and is CRYSTALLINE at room temperature. In sodium chloride, the ions are held together in a lattice which is cubic in shape.

As is also usual with ionic compounds, sodium chloride will dissolve in water to form a SOLUTION which conducts electricity (see page 26).

Magnesium oxide (see page 36) and iron(II) sulphide are other ionic compounds.

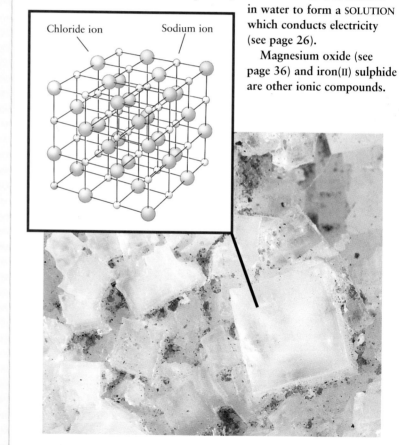

Chloride ion   Sodium ion

8

Chemical stability of compounds

Compounds formed from the more reactive elements are more stable than compounds of the less reactive elements.

Very reactive elements, such as chlorine and sodium, form compounds with strong bonds that are difficult to break, and the resulting compound is relatively stable (see page 10). On the other hand, if the compound is made of elements that are relatively unreactive, the bonds formed will be weaker and, as a result, the compound will be much less stable.

Mercury(II) oxide, for example, will readily decompose on heating (see page 18).

Naming compounds and their occurrence

Compounds ending in **-ide** contain two elements (iron(II) sulphide is a compound of iron and sulphur (FeS)). Compounds ending in **-ite** or **-ate** contain oxygen. There is a greater proportion of oxygen in the compounds ending in **-ate**. Sodium nitrate, $NaNO_3$, and sodium nitrite, $NaNO_2$ (see page 21) are compounds of sodium and nitrogen with different proportions of oxygen.

Of all the known compounds on Earth, 95% contain carbon and are called ORGANIC compounds. However, the most common compounds by mass on our planet do not contain carbon and are called inorganic compounds. These are the MINERALS that make up the Earth's rocks, and water.

The most reactive elements are the ALKALI METALS in Group 1, at the left-hand side of the Periodic Table, along with non-metals such as the HALOGENS (e.g. chlorine), sulphur and oxygen in Groups 6 and 7 towards the right of the Periodic Table. As a result, many of the compounds found on Earth contain these elements as metal oxides, sulphides, sulphates, sulphides and chlorides.

Carbon is a very common element, also found in an INORGANIC form as carbonates. It is also commonly found bonded with hydrogen, nitrogen, oxygen, and other elements in forming millions of organic compounds, which are the building blocks of life.

COVALENT BONDS

(*Left*) Methane gas is a compound in which the component elements are covalently bonded. Covalent bonds are formed when atoms combine by sharing electrons to give a more stable structure. They most commonly occur when non-metal elements bond together.

Other covalently bonded compounds include water, ammonia, hydrogen chloride and carbon dioxide. The structures formed by covalent bonding are called MOLECULES (not ions). Certain elements may exist as molecules in which the atoms are held together by covalent bonds. Examples include oxygen (O_2), chlorine (Cl_2), nitrogen (N_2) and hydrogen (H_2).

Many gases are compounds with covalent bonds and have molecular structures. Many gases are molecular compounds.

Hydrogen atom

Carbon atom

Obtaining elements from their compounds

As the demonstrations on the following pages show, there are many ways of obtaining elements from their compounds. Compounds can be broken down using heat (see pages 18 to 21) in a process known as THERMAL DECOMPOSITION or by using electricity in a process called ELECTROLYSIS (see pages 26 to 32). Compounds can also be broken down using REDUCTION (see pages 22 to 25) and by LEACHING, (dissolving them in a solvent). Each method has considerable practical application, especially in the field of metal refining, because the great majority of the world's metals are found as compounds, usually chlorides, sulphides, oxides and carbonates.

All of the less reactive metals form ores which are insoluble compounds. Pyrite (iron sulphide), is perhaps the best known of the sulphides. Other sulphide ores include galena (lead sulphide), sphalerite (zinc sulphide) and chalcopyrite (copper sulphide).

By contrast, many of the highly reactive metals form compounds that are soluble. These are chiefly compounds of the chlorides. Sodium chloride (common salt, or rock salt), for example, is found dissolved in all the freshwater rivers and lakes of the world as well as in the sea!

Nitrates have not been mentioned so far. They are so easily dissolved that they are uncommon compounds in nature. Most nitrate compounds are found in extremely dry deserts or have to be produced by chemical reactions.

INDUSTRIAL EXTRACTION USING ELECTROLYSIS

(Below) In the industrial production of chlorine, sodium chloride as BRINE (a concentrated solution of common salt), is separated using electrolysis. An electric current is passed through an electrolytic cell containing the sodium chloride. The cell is divided in half by a SEMIPERMEABLE MEMBRANE designed to allow sodium ions to pass through, but not the larger chloride ions.

The chloride ions lose electrons to become chlorine atoms, which then combine together in pairs to form chlorine gas molecules, which can bubble out of the brine and be collected.

Because industrial processes have to be as efficient as possible, the cell is arranged to collect not just chlorine, but also the important chemicals, hydrogen gas and sodium hydroxide (caustic soda).

The electrolysis of brine in the laboratory is shown on page 26.

EQUATION: Electrolysis of a salt solution
Sodium chloride + water ⇨ sodium hydroxide + chlorine + hydrogen
$$2NaCl(aq) + 2H_2O(l) \Rightarrow 2NaOH(aq) + Cl_2(g) + H_2(g)$$
Electrical energy

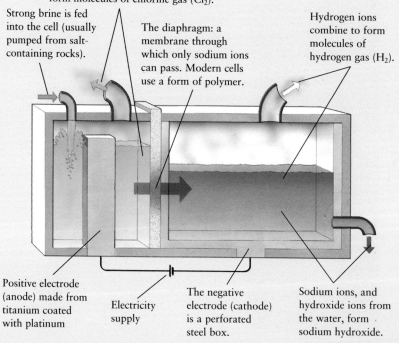

Chloride ions are converted to chlorine atoms which form molecules of chlorine gas (Cl_2).

Strong brine is fed into the cell (usually pumped from salt-containing rocks).

The diaphragm: a membrane through which only sodium ions can pass. Modern cells use a form of polymer.

Hydrogen ions combine to form molecules of hydrogen gas (H_2).

Positive electrode (anode) made from titanium coated with platinum

Electricity supply

The negative electrode (cathode) is a perforated steel box.

Sodium ions, and hydroxide ions from the water, form sodium hydroxide.

(*Right*) Aluminium is a reactive metal and occurs naturally as compounds. In particular, it is found as aluminium oxide, in BAUXITE ore. In the industrial extraction of the metal from this ore, an oxide of aluminium called alumina is first formed. However, this compound requires a lot more energy to separate into its component aluminium and oxygen.

In an industrial refinery, aluminium is extracted from alumina by electrolysis in what is called the Hall–Héroult process.

Hundreds of steel-cased cells (called electrolytic cells or pots) are used. Each cell uses a mere 4 to 6 V (volts), which is about the same as a dry cell uses for a torch, but the current that flows is sometimes as much as 150,000 A (amperes).

The alumina has to be liquefied so that it will DISSOCIATE (break apart) into its component elements as ions. This is done by dissolving the alumina in molten cryolite in the cell at 980°C. The cryolite lowers the melting point of the alumina, thus saving electricity.

Carbon (graphite) electrodes are dipped into the molten mixture, and the current is passed through the cell. The electrical energy forces the alumina to dissociate into aluminium ions and oxide ions.

The aluminium ions, which have a positive charge, move through the liquid to gather at the negatively charged electrode of the cell (the CATHODE).

The oxygen ions move to the positively charged electrode (the ANODE), reacting with the carbon to form carbon dioxide gas.

This process operates continuously, the molten aluminium being siphoned out of the cells and new alumina added from above. The aluminium can then be fed to mills and rolled into sheets, poured into moulds where it cools to make ingots for later use, or mixed with other metals to make ALLOYS.

EQUATION: Overall equation for the reduction of alumina to aluminium
Alumina ⇨ *aluminium + oxygen*
$$2Al_2O_3(s) \Rightarrow 4Al(s) + 3O_2(g)$$

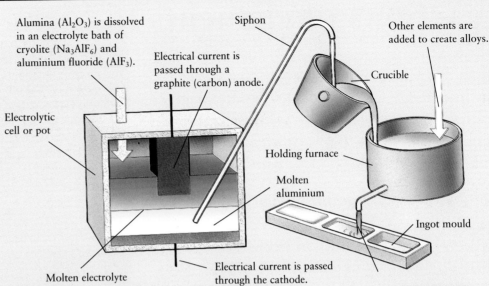

Alumina (Al_2O_3) is dissolved in an electrolyte bath of cryolite (Na_3AlF_6) and aluminium fluoride (AlF_3).

Electrical current is passed through a graphite (carbon) anode.

Siphon

Other elements are added to create alloys.

Crucible

Electrolytic cell or pot

Holding furnace

Molten aluminium

Molten electrolyte

Electrical current is passed through the cathode.

Ingot mould

Aluminium is being poured into moulds to make ingots.

(*Above*) White alumina powder

(*Above right*) A cell being operated in the cell room. Molten aluminium is siphoned into the pot attached to the cell in the foreground.
(*Right*) Pouring molten aluminium into moulds.

Reactions of elements to form compounds

Some elements react together to form compounds. This happens in the atmosphere, for example, when a metal corrodes. The metal may combine with oxygen from the air. However, the formation of a compound can be spectacular during combustion, as can be seen in the next three demonstrations.

Demonstration 1: combining carbon and oxygen

A supply of oxygen is prepared by pouring hydrogen peroxide on to manganese dioxide in a flask. The oxygen is collected in a gas jar over water. A small depth of limewater is poured into the bottom of the jar, where it remains colourless.

A piece of carbon in the form of charcoal is gripped in a pair of metal tongs and heated strongly in a Bunsen flame (①). When the charcoal begins to glow, it is held in the gas jar of oxygen (②).

The combustion of the carbon produces an intense white light but no flames. The reaction also produces a compound – covalently bonded molecules of carbon dioxide gas.

Once the combustion has finished, the charcoal is taken out and the cover slip is quickly replaced. The gas jar is shaken and the limewater immediately turns cloudy showing the presence of carbon dioxide gas (③). White, insoluble, calcium carbonate has been precipitated as a suspension, and it is this that is seen as a 'cloudiness' in the limewater.

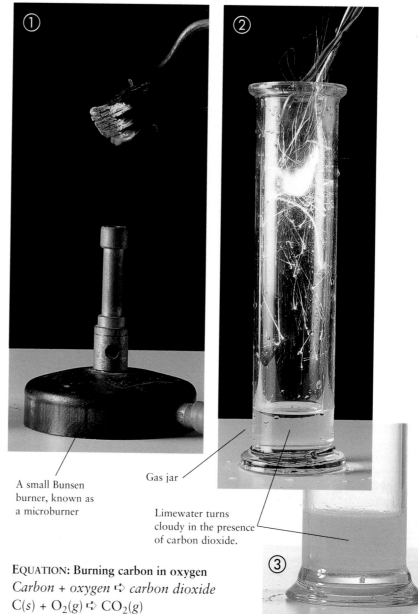

① ②

A small Bunsen burner, known as a microburner

Gas jar

Limewater turns cloudy in the presence of carbon dioxide.

③

EQUATION: Burning carbon in oxygen
Carbon + oxygen ⇨ carbon dioxide
$C(s) + O_2(g) \Rightarrow CO_2(g)$

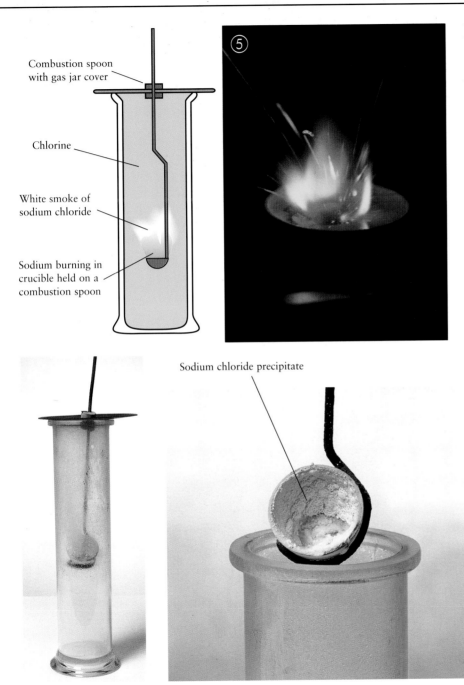

Combustion spoon with gas jar cover

Chlorine

White smoke of sodium chloride

Sodium burning in crucible held on a combustion spoon

⑤

Sodium chloride precipitate

Demonstration 2: combining sodium and chlorine

A supply of chlorine is prepared in a fume chamber by reacting concentrated hydrochloric acid with potassium permanganate. As chlorine is denser than air, the greenish-yellow gas can be collected by upward displacement of air.

A very small pellet of sodium is next placed in a crucible, which is held on a COMBUSTION SPOON and heated strongly in a Bunsen flame until it begins to burn. At this stage, the spoon is plunged into the gas jar of chlorine. (④).

The sodium burns in the chlorine with a yellow flame (⑤). At the same time, a white smoke is formed in the gas jar (⑥) and a white solid accumulates in the crucible (⑦). The smoke and the solid in the spoon are both particles of sodium chloride, the compound formed by the reaction of the two elements. Sodium chloride is an ionic compound (see page 8) and is the principal constituent of table salt. (Note: the sodium chloride produced should *not* be tasted because it has not been formed in hygienic conditions.)

EQUATION: Burning sodium in chlorine
Sodium + chlorine ⇨ sodium chloride
$2Na(s) + Cl_2(g) ⇨ 2NaCl(s)$

Demonstration 3: combining bromine and aluminium

Bromine is poisonous and so this demonstration is performed in a fume chamber. Some shiny aluminium foil is cut into thin strips to produce a large surface area of metal for the bromine to react with. The strips are placed on a watch glass (⑧). A few drops of bromine are then dripped on to the aluminium, and the laboratory lights dimmed. Within a few seconds, dense smoke issues from the reactants, and a few seconds later the heat generated is sufficient for combustion to take place and for the reactants to glow brightly with a red and orange light (⑨).

When the reaction is over, a grey powder is left on the watch glass and surrounding surface (⑩). This is the ionic compound, aluminium bromide.

EQUATION: **Burning aluminium in bromine**
Aluminium + bromine ⇨ Aluminium bromide
$2Al(s) + 3Br_2(g) ⇨ 2AlBr_3(s)$

⑨

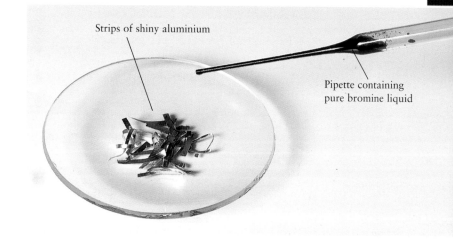

Strips of shiny aluminium

Pipette containing pure bromine liquid

14

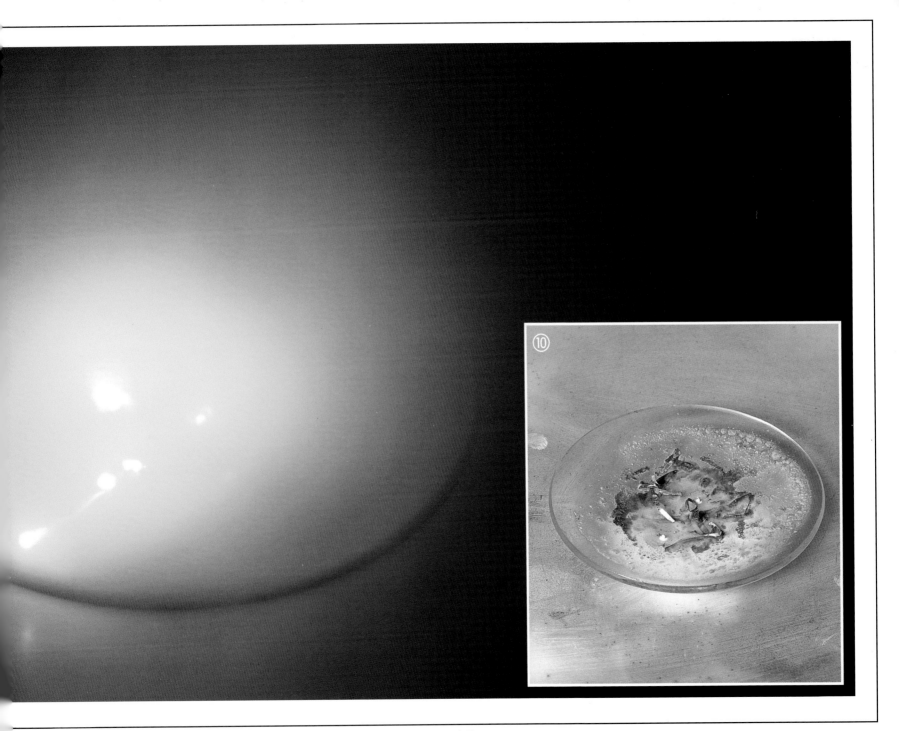

Comparing compounds with their elements

Compounds do not have the same properties as the elements from which they are made. This demonstration uses elements with well-recognised and easily identified properties to investigate how they differ from the compound they make.

Demonstration: investigating the properties of sulphur, iron and iron(II) sulphide

In this demonstration, the elements iron and sulphur are used. The iron is in the form of iron filings, and the sulphur is a yellow powder (①).

At room temperature, these elements can be mixed and no reaction will take place. In a mixture, the two elements retain their separate properties. A mixture can be separated by physical means and, in this case, the magnetic properties of the iron allow the filings to be removed using a magnet (see page 55). A yellow powder of sulphur is left behind.

If the mixture is placed in a test tube (②) and heated in a Bunsen flame, a reaction between the elements is started that, itself, gives out heat. This is seen by the red glow (③). Such a reaction is called EXOTHERMIC. In this case, the reaction carries on even when the test tube is removed from the Bunsen flame. The glowing section in which the reaction is taking place passes up the test tube until complete.

The product of the reaction between these two elements is iron(II) sulphide, a metallic brown-coloured compound (④) that looks very different from the original elements. Most significantly the iron(II) sulphide has no magnetic properties. As is also characteristic of a compound, the iron(II) sulphide is not easily separated into its component elements.

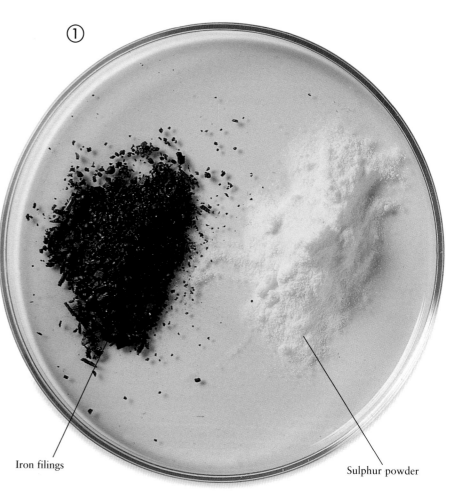

①

Iron filings

Sulphur powder

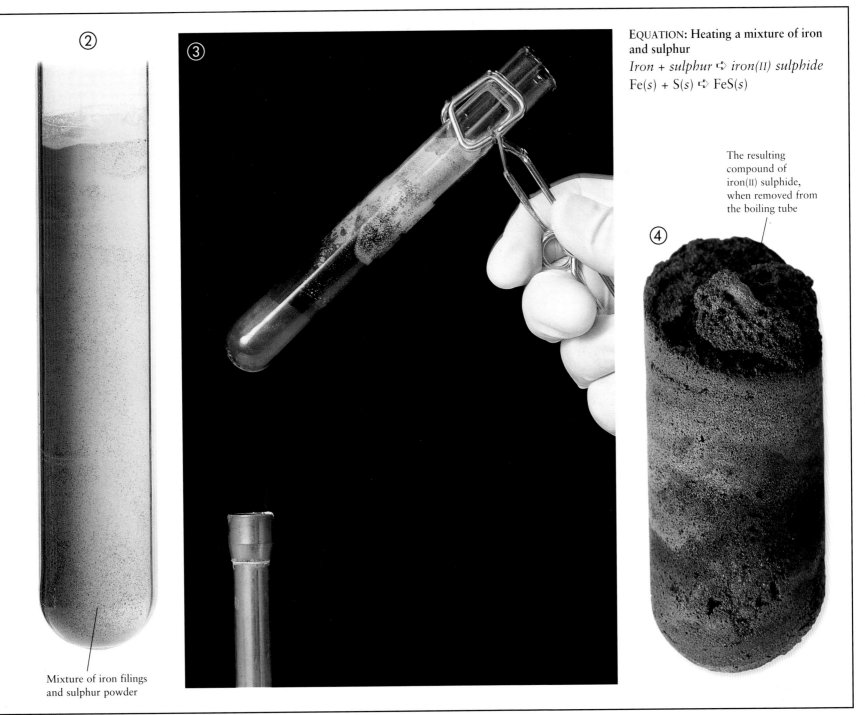

② Mixture of iron filings and sulphur powder

③ EQUATION: **Heating a mixture of iron and sulphur**

Iron + sulphur ⇨ *iron(II) sulphide*

$Fe(s) + S(s) ⇨ FeS(s)$

④ The resulting compound of iron(II) sulphide, when removed from the boiling tube

Obtaining elements from their compounds by thermal decomposition

Metals vary widely in their reactivity. The most reactive metals produce compounds which are hardest to separate back into their elements, whereas the least reactive metals produce compounds that decompose back to their elements relatively easily.

The more reactive elements are at the top of the REACTIVITY SERIES (①), while the least reactive elements are towards the bottom. In the four demonstrations that follow, we shall investigate how far compounds of the less reactive and the more reactive metals can be decomposed back to their elements by heating – a process known as thermal decomposition.

②

③

Demonstration 1: thermal decomposition of mercury(II) oxide

Mercury is so low down the reactive series that one of its compounds, mercury(II) oxide (HgO) is totally decomposed by heating. Its component elements of the metal and oxygen are separated on moderate heating.

As mercury vapour is poisonous, this demonstration is performed in a fume chamber.

Red mercury(II) oxide (HgO) (②) is heated in a boiling tube. Within a few minutes the powder turns black and begins to decompose into mercury and oxygen gas (③).

① REACTIVITY SERIES	
Element	*Reactivity*
potassium	*most reactive*
sodium	
calcium	
magnesium	
aluminium	
manganese	
chromium	
zinc	
iron	
cadmium	
tin	
lead	
hydrogen	
copper	
mercury	
silver	
gold	
platinum	*least reactive*

④

EQUATION: Heating mercury(II) oxide
Mercury(II) oxide ⇨ mercury + oxygen
$HgO(s) \Rightarrow Hg(s) + O_2(g)$

The mercury boils and condenses on to the colder region near the mouth of the tube, where it forms droplets of mercury (④) that may form a mercury mirror.

The presence of oxygen can be tested for by placing a glowing splint inside the mouth of the tube and watching as it is rekindled.

Demonstration 2: thermal decomposition of lead nitrate

Mercury(II) oxide is exceptional because heating decomposes it into both of its component elements in one stage. Most compounds are only partly decomposed on heating, and can only be completely decomposed by more complex means. For example, if a powder of white lead nitrate is placed in a boiling tube and heated (⑤), it changes colour to orange and then yellow, first as it melts and then as it decomposes to lead oxide.

The bubbles and the brown fumes are a mixture of oxygen and nitrogen dioxide gases (⑥). The elemental oxygen can be separated from this mixture by passing the gases through a cooling bath to liquefy the nitrogen dioxide. Oxygen can also be tested for by using a glowing splint, which will be rekindled.

Remarks

Partly decomposing a metal compound to convert it to its oxide is a technique widely used in metal refining. It is often referred to as ROASTING. The oxygen of the air may be involved in this type of treatment.

To obtain elemental metal, however, the metal oxide must be reduced (see pages 10, 22 to 25 and 29).

⑤

⑥

EQUATION: Decomposition of lead nitrate
Lead nitrate ⇨ lead oxide + nitrogen dioxide + oxygen
$2Pb(NO_3)_2(s) \Rightarrow 2PbO(s) + 4NO_2(g) + O_2(g)$

Demonstration 3: thermal decomposition of zinc nitrate

Zinc is slightly more reactive than lead, and therefore its compounds are even more reluctant to decompose into its elements.

If crystals of zinc nitrate are heated in a boiling tube, the colourless crystals (⑦) first melt and give off WATER OF CRYSTALLISATION as steam (⑧). The zinc nitrate liquid is heated further until it decomposes into bright yellow zinc oxide (⑨), while giving off brown nitrogen dioxide gas (⑩) and oxygen. The oxygen rekindles a glowing splint (⑪ and ⑫) and is the only element separated. The zinc oxide and the nitrogen dioxide are both compounds.

It is difficult to reduce zinc oxide to zinc metal by heating it with carbon in the method shown for lead oxide on page 22.

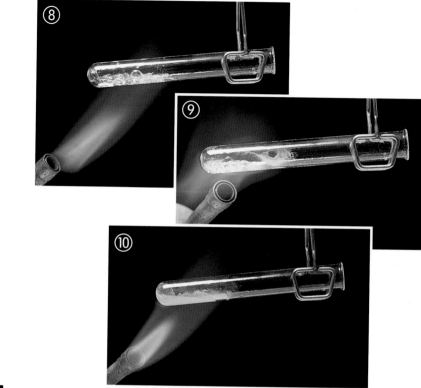

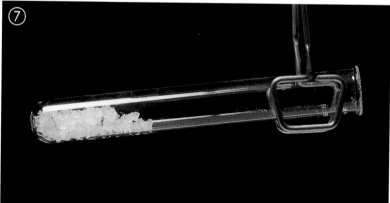

EQUATION: Heating zinc nitrate

Zinc nitrate ⇨ zinc oxide + nitrogen dioxide + oxygen

$2Zn(NO_3)_2(s) \Rightarrow 2ZnO(s) + 4NO_2(g) + O_2(g)$

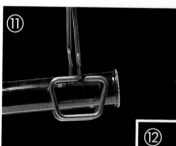

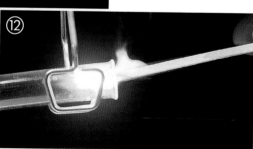

Demonstration 4: thermal decomposition of sodium nitrate

Sodium is a much more reactive metal than zinc and so its compounds are even more difficult to decompose than zinc compounds.

When a small amount of sodium nitrate powder is placed in a boiling tube and then heated (⑬), it first melts to produce a greenish-yellow liquid (sodium nitrite) and it bubbles as oxygen gas is given off (⑭). The presence of oxygen is proved by rekindling a glowing splint (⑮).

In this case, the nitrate does not decompose to an oxide, and nitrogen dioxide is not given off. Sodium nitrite cannot be decomposed by further heating and, when the heat is removed, it eventually cools to a white solid of sodium nitrite.

Remarks

Because the compounds of more reactive metals do not decompose as readily as those made from metals low down the reactivity series, they are far more difficult to refine. Industrial refining usually uses electrical energy to isolate the metal from its compound (see pages 10 and 30). However, for laboratory purposes, this property can be put to good use. Nitrates of reactive metals can conveniently be used to generate small amounts of oxygen for demonstration purposes.

EQUATION: Heating sodium nitrate
Sodium nitrate ⇨ sodium nitrite + oxygen
$2NaNO_3(s) ⇨ 2NaNO_2(s) + O_2(g)$

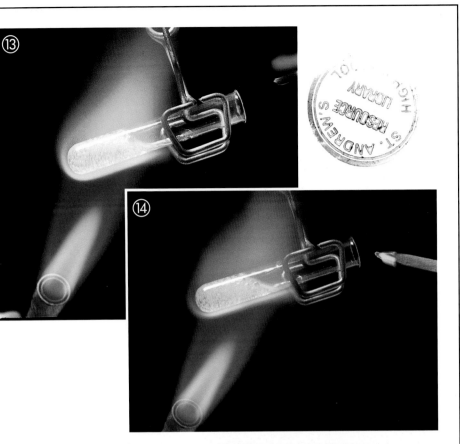

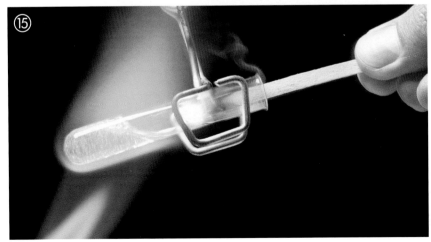

Obtaining elements from their compounds using a reducing agent

REDUCTION is the chemical reaction in which some or all of the oxygen is removed from a compound containing oxygen. It is the most important process used in industry for REFINING metal oxide ores. Some compounds may have to be converted to an oxide in a preliminary stage.

To reduce a metal oxide, a number of reducing agents can be used, the most common being carbon and carbon monoxide.

In a BLAST FURNACE for making iron, for example, iron oxide is reduced at high temperatures to elemental iron using carbon monoxide. However, this is difficult to do in a laboratory, because such high temperatures are required.

Demonstration 1: reduction of lead(II) oxide

In this demonstration, an orange form of lead(II) oxide (lead monoxide) known as litharge is used.

Lead is low down the reactivity series (see page 18) and so lead compounds are decomposed or reduced relatively easily. The lower temperatures required make lead compounds more suitable for use in this laboratory demonstration than compounds of the more reactive metals such as iron (see page 24).

Carbon, in the form of a charcoal block, is used as the reducing agent here. A hollow is made in the

Heat applied

Orange lead(II) oxide powder (litharge)

Yellow lead(II) oxide powder (massicote)

①

Carbon block

charcoal block, to act as the reducing crucible for the lead(II) oxide and to contain the lead when it becomes molten during the reaction.

A small amount of lead(II) oxide powder is placed in the hollowed-out part of the charcoal block, and a Bunsen flame is used to heat it (①). To start with, the litharge turns yellow as it forms another form of lead(II) oxide called massicote (②).

However, as the temperature is increased, the carbon reacts with, and reduces, the lead(II) oxide.

EQUATION: Reduction of lead monoxide
Lead(II) oxide + carbon ⇨ lead + carbon monoxide
$2PbO(s) + 2C(s) ⇨ 2Pb(s) + 2CO(g)$

②

③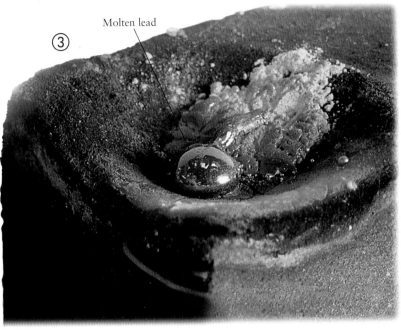

Molten lead

④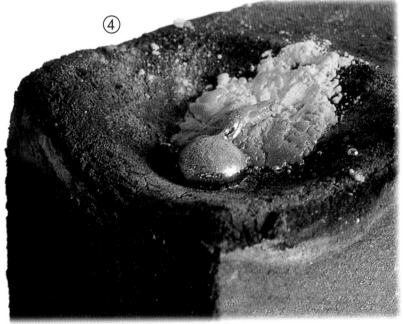

Elemental lead is separated and forms a molten globule (③), which steadily grows. The carbon is oxidised to colourless carbon monoxide and then carbon dioxide gas, which disperse into the surrounding air.

The molten globule will form solid lead if left to cool (④), and does not readily oxidise in the oxygen of the atmosphere to re-form lead oxide, although the surface becomes dull as a new, thin layer of oxide forms.

Demonstration 2: reduction of iron(II) oxide

Iron is a more reactive element than lead, forming compounds that are more difficult to decompose or reduce. The iron in iron(II) oxide cannot be reduced to elemental iron with the heat of a Bunsen flame. For the reduction process to work, temperatures over 1800°C are required, and these can only be obtained in a special furnace, or by setting in motion a chemical reaction that releases sufficient heat (is sufficiently exothermic) to reduce the iron.

Because it is impossible to get high furnace temperatures in most laboratories, most small-scale demonstrations use a chemical reaction that generates large amounts of heat. Even so, this demonstration cannot be done inside a laboratory.

The iron(II) oxide is placed in a suitable earthenware plant pot as a container (which will be destroyed), together with powdered aluminium. Some barium peroxide is placed in a hollow formed in the surface of this mixture, and a fuse of magnesium ribbon is pushed into the barium peroxide (⑤).

The whole apparatus is placed out in a field, well away from any FLAMMABLE materials and spectators. The magnesium fuse is then lit and the magnesium begins to burn with a brilliant white light (⑥).

The fuse quickly burns down into the barium peroxide, and the heat causes the barium peroxide to decompose and release oxygen. At this stage, the demonstration resembles a Roman candle firework.

Enough heat energy is produced by this reaction to raise the temperature of the aluminium powder sufficiently for it to react with the oxygen in the iron(II) oxide. The iron(II) oxide is reduced to molten, liquid, elemental iron. This is a highly exothermic

⑤

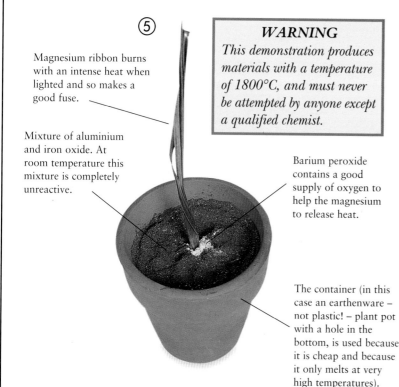

Magnesium ribbon burns with an intense heat when lighted and so makes a good fuse.

Mixture of aluminium and iron oxide. At room temperature this mixture is completely unreactive.

Barium peroxide contains a good supply of oxygen to help the magnesium to release heat.

The container (in this case an earthenware – not plastic! – plant pot with a hole in the bottom, is used because it is cheap and because it only melts at very high temperatures).

> ### WARNING
> *This demonstration produces materials with a temperature of 1800°C, and must never be attempted by anyone except a qualified chemist.*

⑥

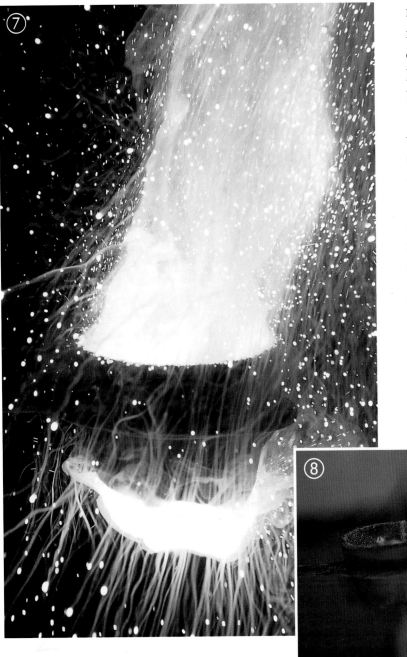

reaction producing even more heat, so that the molten metal reaches in excess of 1800°C. The high temperature cracks the container at its base, and the heavy, molten, liquid, elemental iron sinks through the mixture and can be seen pouring and splattering from the cracks (⑦).

The molten iron is collected safely in a dish filled with water and sand. The water in the container goes up in steam as soon as the iron flows into it, adding to the spectacular effect (⑧).

Whilst the iron(II) oxide is reduced, the aluminium is oxidised to aluminium oxide. The aluminium oxide is a lightweight, fine powder that is easily carried aloft, as a white smoke, by the rising currents of hot air.

Remarks

Iron oxides are the iron compounds used in iron SMELTING. In a blast furnace used for smelting, carbon monoxide is used as the reducing agent. The carbon monoxide is generated inside the furnace by the combustion of carbon (in the form of coke) in a limited supply of oxygen. The iron oxide compound is reduced to molten, liquid, elemental iron that can be drained off. At the same time, the carbon monoxide is oxidised to carbon dioxide.

EQUATION: Reduction of iron oxide to iron
Iron(II) oxide + aluminium ⇨ iron + aluminium oxide
$Fe_2O_3(s) + 2Al(s) \Rightarrow 2Fe(s) + Al_2O_3(s)$

Obtaining elements from their compounds by electrolysis of solutions in water

Compounds of the more reactive metals (see page 18) are difficult to separate into their elements by decomposition or by heating with reducing agents. They can often be separated when electricity is passed through them, in a liquid state, in a process called electrolysis. As a result, electrolysis is widely used in industry for obtaining the most reactive metals (e.g. sodium), for refining metals (e.g. copper), and for producing other elements such as chlorine (see page 10).

Electrolysis uses electrical energy to break up an ELECTROLYTE. An electrolyte is a liquid that will react chemically when electricity is passed through it. A low-voltage, direct current, electricity supply is used.

Compounds such as sodium chloride and copper sulphate contain ions (see page 8), and can be dissolved in water (a solvent) to form a solution that is an electrolyte. The next two demonstrations illustrate this.

Demonstration 1: electrolysis of sodium chloride solution

A solution of sodium chloride is made by dissolving sodium chloride (table salt) in distilled water. This solution, called brine, is colourless and so UNIVERSAL INDICATOR is added to allow the observer to see some

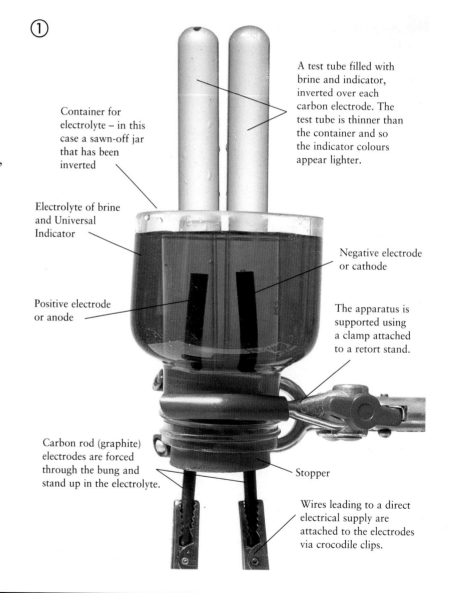

①

Container for electrolyte – in this case a sawn-off jar that has been inverted

A test tube filled with brine and indicator, inverted over each carbon electrode. The test tube is thinner than the container and so the indicator colours appear lighter.

Electrolyte of brine and Universal Indicator

Negative electrode or cathode

Positive electrode or anode

The apparatus is supported using a clamp attached to a retort stand.

Carbon rod (graphite) electrodes are forced through the bung and stand up in the electrolyte.

Stopper

Wires leading to a direct electrical supply are attached to the electrodes via crocodile clips.

of the results of the electrolysis. The brine is neutral and the indicator is green.

Some of the sodium chloride solution is poured into a container with ELECTRODES. In this case, the apparatus has been constructed from the sawn-off top of a jar with a rubber stopper (①). Two carbon (graphite) rods are used as electrodes and are pushed through holes made in the stopper.

The electrodes stand up vertically in the electrolyte. This design allows test tubes filled with the brine and indicator solution to be inverted over the electrodes. Care is taken not to allow air to enter the tubes. Any gases given off during electrolysis are collected in these tubes. The use of glassware also

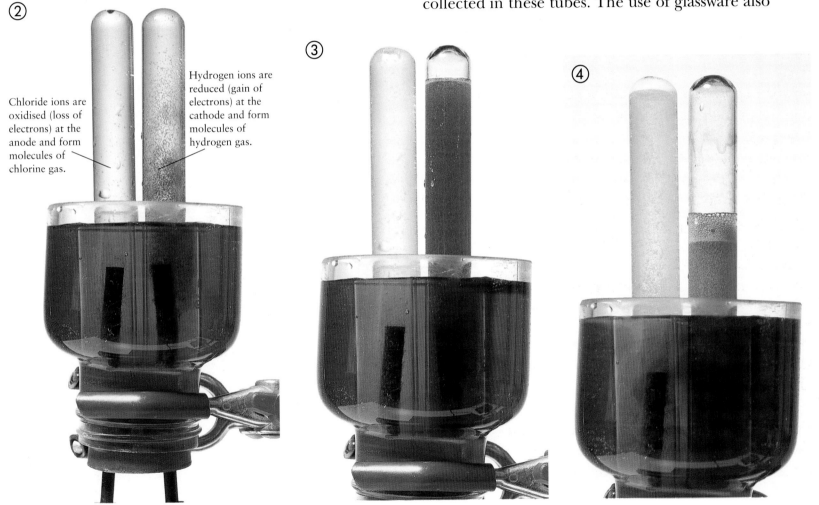

②

Chloride ions are oxidised (loss of electrons) at the anode and form molecules of chlorine gas.

Hydrogen ions are reduced (gain of electrons) at the cathode and form molecules of hydrogen gas.

③

④

allows a clear view of what is happening during the electrolysis. (Note: various designs of apparatus may be used for electrolysis. Each performs the same function equally well.)

Crocodile clips connect the electrodes to a direct current electrical supply which is now switched on. A current will flow through the solution between the electrodes.

The indicator in the tube over the negative electrode immediately turns violet, indicating that the solution is becoming alkaline. This is caused by sodium hydroxide being formed. Vigorous effervescence also occurs, which is hydrogen gas being given off (②).

Meanwhile, bubbles of gas are also given off at the positive electrode and rise up the tube, turning the indicator slightly yellow (③). This acidic solution is caused by chlorine gas. Chlorine is soluble and so is dissolved in the water until SATURATED, taking some time to accumulate at the top of the tube. The chlorine can be seen because it is green. It also bleaches the test solution in the test tube (④).

As a further test that chlorine has been separated from the sodium chloride, the tube containing the bleached solution is removed carefully from the apparatus whilst being sealed with a finger. A piece of filter paper soaked in colourless potassium iodide is then placed close to the open end of the tube (⑤) and the gas allowed to escape (⑥ and (⑦). The instant brown colouration to the filter paper is a test for a strong OXIDISING AGENT, which chlorine is.

Remarks

If gases effervesce rapidly from the electrodes, water might not be displaced evenly from the base of the tubes, causing the tubes to rock and possibly topple over. To prevent this problem, the tubes can be clamped and held with their bases slightly clear of the bung. If the tubes fit too well on the base, this may also restrict the movement of ions and so slow down the rate of electrolysis. The problem is reduced by using a lower electrical current.

HALF EQUATION: Chloride ions from the sodium chloride solution are reduced to chlorine atoms by electrolysis. They then pair up into chlorine molecules.

Chloride ions ⇨ chlorine molecules + electrons

$$2Cl^-(aq) \Rightarrow Cl_2(g) + 2e^-$$

Electric current

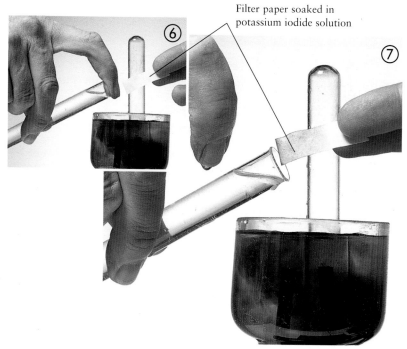

Filter paper soaked in potassium iodide solution

Demonstration 2: purifying copper by electrolysis

This demonstration shows, in miniature, one of the most common industrial processes for PURIFYING a metal by electrolysis. Most pure copper is obtained in this way.

Reagent quality copper sulphate solution is used as the electrolyte and is poured into a glass bath. Two similar, curled sheets of copper are used as electrodes and are held against the glass and in solution using crocodile clips. These are, in turn, connected with wires to a direct current electrical supply pack (⑧).

When the electrical power supply is switched on, copper ions are formed at the anode and transferred to the solution, while copper ions are converted into copper metal at the cathode.

The first signs of this reaction occur within the first minute of the demonstration, as both electrodes change colour (⑨). The anode on the right begins to look shiny, simply because it is losing copper from its surface. It is common for the copper eventually to corrode right through and develop holes.

At the same time, the cathode on the left is plated in elemental copper and it becomes more orange-looking. Soon, fern-like deposits of copper develop in the direction of the flow of the ions.

During this reaction, the transfer of ions has no overall effect on the concentration of copper ions in the solution, and the solution remains the same intensity of blue throughout the demonstration.

Remarks

The rate of change at the electrodes depends on the current supplied by the power pack, and some experimentation is needed to get an appropriate speed of electrolysis.

> HALF EQUATION 1: Copper ions are formed at the anode
> *Copper* ⇨ *copper ions + electrons*
> $Cu(s) \Rightarrow Cu^{2+}(aq) + 2e^{-}$
> Electric current
>
> HALF EQUATION 2: Copper metal is formed at the cathode
> *Copper ions + electrons* ⇨ *copper atoms*
> $Cu^{2+}(aq) + 2e^{-} \Rightarrow Cu(s)$
> Electric current

Negative electrode or cathode

Positive electrode or anode

Obtaining elements from molten compounds by electrolysis

Some compounds that are solid at room temperature can be heated into molten liquid that can be separated by electrolysis. In this demonstration, lead bromide is melted to show that it will then become an electrolyte. Lead bromide is used because it has a low melting point. The same principle of electrolytic refining is used in industry to obtain metals from molten compounds of elements such as aluminium and sodium.

Demonstration: electrolysis of molten lead bromide

Two stages are necessary for this demonstration.

First, some lead bromide is placed in a boiling tube and heated until it becomes molten. A rubber bung with two carbon-rod electrodes can then be lowered into the molten lead bromide and the apparatus allowed to cool. Now an electric current must be passed between the electrodes to perform the electrolysis.

To see how well solid lead bromide conducts electricity, the electrodes are connected in a SERIES CIRCUIT with a power pack and a light bulb. With the power pack switched on, there is no illumination from the bulb (①), showing that the circuit is not electrically complete. No electrolysis can take place, and the solid remains unaltered.

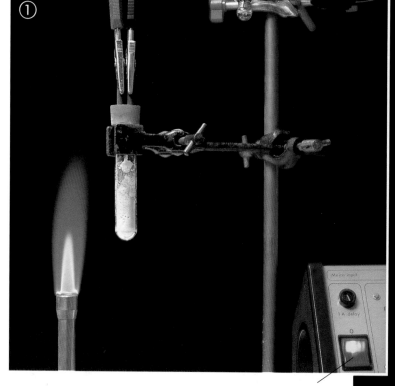

Unlit bulb

Power pack switched on

HALF EQUATION 1: Lead ions form lead atoms at the cathode
Lead ions + electrons ⇨ lead atoms
$Pb^{2+}(l) + 2e^- \Rightarrow Pb(l)$
Electric current

HALF EQUATION 2: Bromide ions form bromine atoms which combine to form bromine molecules (gas) at the anode
Bromide ions ⇨ bromine molecules + electrons
$2Br^-(l) \Rightarrow Br_2(g) + 2e^-$
Electric current

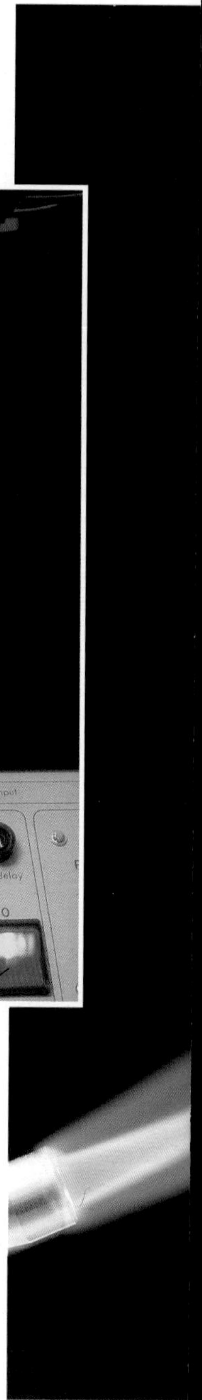

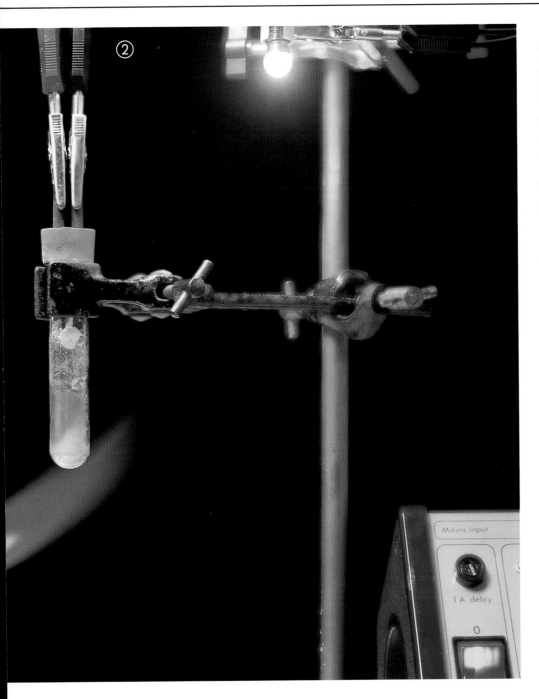

As the lead bromide is heated using a Bunsen flame, it appears to become liquid, but the bulb still does not light. This is because, as non-metal solids conduct heat slowly, the lead bromide near the source of heating can be molten, while the lead bromide between the electrodes remains solid. However, when all of the solid is molten, the bulb lights up, indicating that the circuit is complete and that an electric current is flowing through the lead bromide (②). Under these circumstances, as with the solutions on pages 22 and 25, an ELECTROLYTIC CELL has been formed, and electrolysis can take place.

Bromide ions form brown bromine gas at the positive electrode or anode, which is on the left in this demonstration. Meanwhile, lead ions are discharged and form molten lead metal at the negative electrode or cathode.

Remarks

Because the electrolyte has to be heated and bromine is very toxic, it would be too complicated to try to examine the process of electrolysis any further in the laboratory. The process is halted before a significant amount of bromine is released. However, electrolysis in the molten state has many industrial applications, including refining aluminium (see page 11).

Reactions of an element with a compound

A compound is any substance consisting of more than one element that has a fixed chemical composition. All ACIDS, BASES and SALTS are therefore compounds.

Reactions between elements and compounds may produce new compounds, or new compounds and some component elements.

Among the more common reactions between an element and a compound is the reaction of a metal with an acid. However, acids will not react with non-metal elements. Very few metals will react with ALKALIS, but those, like aluminium, that do, are called AMPHOTERIC elements.

Demonstration 1: copper and fuming nitric acid

Fuming concentrated nitric acid, which is a compound, is poured on to elemental copper in the form of copper turnings (fine shavings of copper that provide a large surface area for fast reaction) (①). Three new compounds are formed during the reaction. The copper is transformed into a blue salt of copper nitrate. This is dissolved in the water that is produced. At the same time, large amounts of brown nitrogen dioxide gas are given off (②).

EQUATION: Copper and fuming nitric acid

Copper + fuming nitric acid ⇨ *copper(II) nitrate + water + nitrogen dioxide*

$Cu(s) + 4HNO_3(l) \Rightarrow Cu(NO_3)_2(s) + 2H_2O(l) + 2NO_2(g)$

Blue

Demonstration 2: aluminium and sodium hydroxide

Sodium hydroxide solution is a strong alkali (a solution of a base in water). When warm sodium hydroxide solution, which is a compound, is poured into a dish of elemental aluminium (③), a reaction takes place immediately (④).

During the reaction, a new compound of sodium aluminate is produced and the element hydrogen is released. The reaction is fierce and exothermic. The heat that is generated turns some of the water in the sodium hydroxide solution into steam. This, along with the hydrogen gas, forms frothy bubbles.

Within a few minutes, the aluminium has been completely CORRODED where it has reacted with the sodium hydroxide, and the base of the dish has disappeared (⑤).

EQUATION: Aluminium and sodium hydroxide
Aluminium + sodium hydroxide + water ⇨ sodium aluminate + hydrogen
$2Al(s) + 2NaOH\ (aq) + 6H_2O(l) ⇨ 2NaAl(OH)_4(aq) + 3H_2(g)$

Reaction of a compound with a compound

There is a vast range of compounds that will react with other compounds, and these reactions can involve covalent molecules or ions in solution. In many cases, what happens depends on how much of each compound is present, as shown by the demonstration below.

Demonstration: ammonia solution with copper(II) sulphate solution

Some blue copper(II) sulphate solution is poured into a test tube (①). Some colourless ammonia solution (ammonium hydroxide) in a pipette is then added drop by drop and the changes observed. Initially, a blue precipitate is formed (②) where the two compounds come in contact and react. The copper ions from the copper(II) sulphate react with the hydroxide ions in the ammonium hydroxide solution to form copper(II) hydroxide.

The test tube is now shaken so that it is filled with precipitate (③). As more ammonia solution is added, it reaches excess. The solid at the top of the test tube begins to re-dissolve and a very dark blue or indigo solution is formed (④). When more ammonia solution is added, and with sufficient shaking, eventually all of the solid re-dissolves (⑤).

The dark blue new compound that has been formed is a copper complex called diaquatetraamminecopper(II) sulphate (⑥).

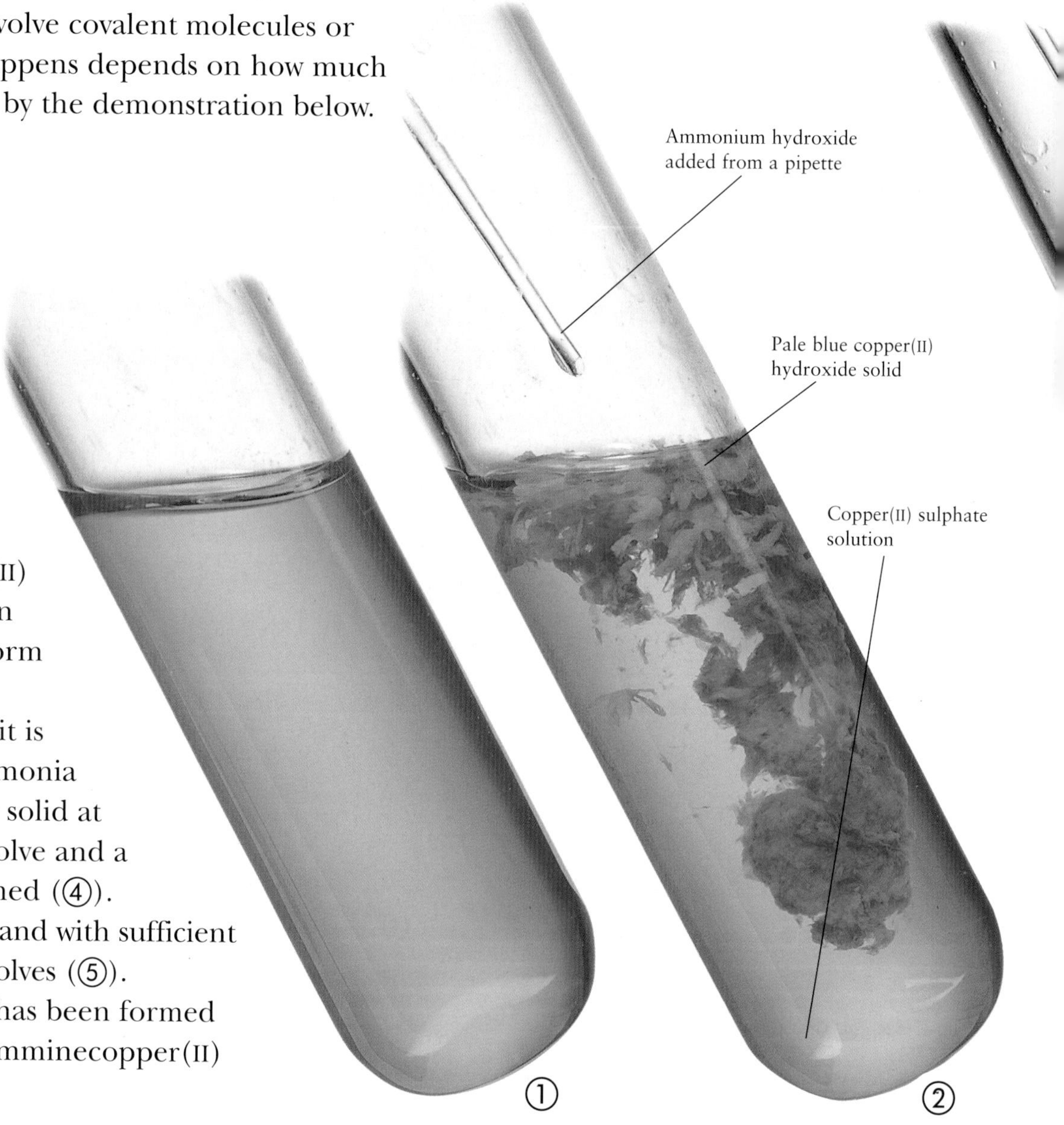

Ammonium hydroxide added from a pipette

Pale blue copper(II) hydroxide solid

Copper(II) sulphate solution

①

②

EQUATION: Initial reaction of ammonium hydroxide and copper(II) sulphate

Ammonium hydroxide + copper(II) sulphate $\Rightarrow$ copper(II) hydroxide + ammonium sulphate

$2NH_4OH(aq) + CuSO_4(aq) \Rightarrow Cu(OH)_2(aq) + (NH_4)_2SO_4(aq)$

EQUATION: Half equation for reaction of excess ammonium hydroxide and copper(II) sulphate

Ammonia + copper(II) ions $\Rightarrow$ diaquatetraamminecopper(II) sulphate

$4NH_3(aq) + Cu^{2+}(aq) \Rightarrow Cu(NH_3)_4{}^{2+}(aq)$

⑥ *(Below)* A representation of a copper complex ion

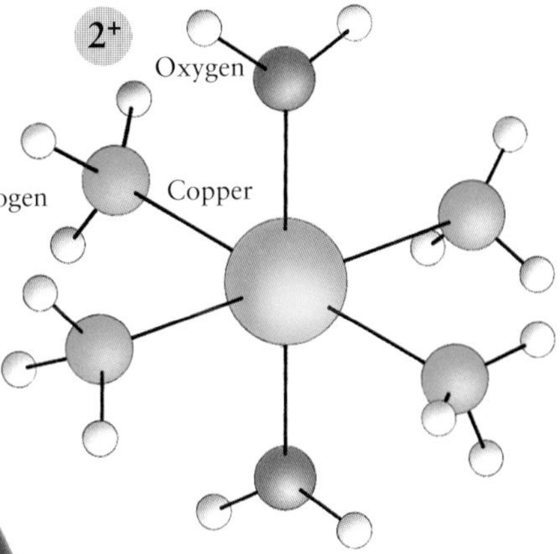

Hydrogen

2+

Oxygen

Nitrogen

Copper

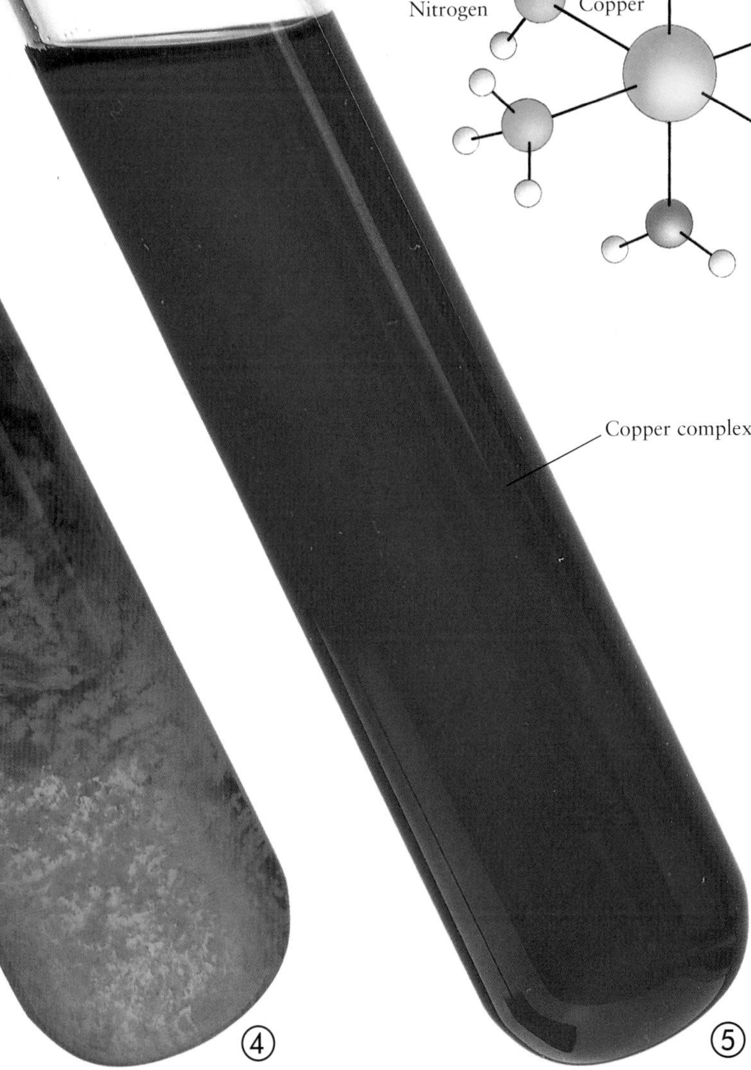

Copper complex

③

④

⑤

Finding the formula of a compound experimentally

In principle, every chemical formula should be able to be determined experimentally. In this demonstration, we show how to calculate the formula of the compound magnesium oxide, and also point out some of the problems that face the unwary.

Demonstration: combustion of magnesium

The apparatus uses a crucible and lid. The objective is to heat the crucible with magnesium inside it until it turns into magnesium oxide. To ensure the magnesium oxidises, it is important to use a loose-fitting lid to the crucible so that air can enter.

Because this is a quantitative demonstration, it is important to weigh the reactants and products, together with their containers, at every stage. At the start of the demonstration, therefore, the crucible and lid are weighed before a strip of magnesium ribbon is placed inside the crucible and is weighed together with its lid. The crucible containing the magnesium strip is placed on a pipe-clay triangle on the tripod, and the lid is placed on top (①). The crucible and its contents are heated over an intense Bunsen flame until they glow red-hot (②).

During the heating, the magnesium reacts with the oxygen in the air to form magnesium oxide (MgO). However, it also reacts with nitrogen in the air to form magnesium nitride (Mg_3N_2). Simple heating does not

Magnesium ribbon

Tripod

Pipe-clay triangle

Crucible and crucible lid

EQUATION: Combustion of magnesium in air
Magnesium + oxygen ⇨ magnesium oxide
$2Mg(s) + O_2(g) ⇨ 2MgO(s)$

produce magnesium oxide on its own, and so further steps must be taken to convert the magnesium nitride to oxide. There is therefore no point in weighing the crucible at this stage because it contains a mixture of magnesium compounds and not a single substance.

The crucible is allowed to cool, and the lid removed (③). Distilled water is now added. The magnesium nitride reacts with the water to form magnesium hydroxide, and at the same time it gives off ammonia gas. The presence of the gas can be tested

Bunsen burner

Magnesium oxide and magnesium nitride

for with damp pH paper (④). Ammonia is an alkaline gas and so turns the pH paper blue (⑤).

To obtain magnesium oxide from the magnesium hydroxide, the lid is placed back on the crucible and the crucible is reheated (⑥). This will drive off the water as steam and DEHYDRATE the magnesium hydroxide to magnesium oxide. The crucible is allowed to cool (⑦) and then it is weighed.

To ensure that all the magnesium hydroxide has been converted to oxide, the crucible is reheated, allowed to cool and then reweighed. If the two weighings produce the same result, the substance in the crucible is magnesium oxide. However, if the weights are different, some magnesium hydroxide still remains and so there must be further heating, cooling and weighing stages until a constant weight is achieved.

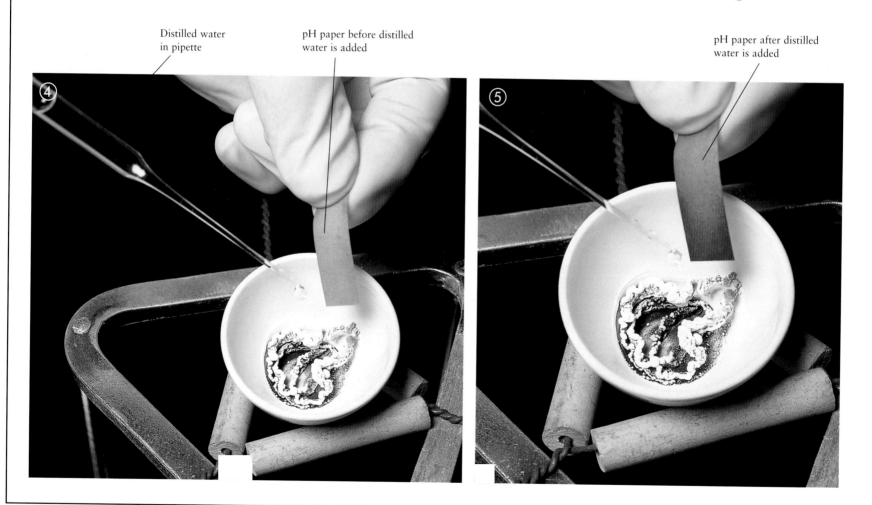

Distilled water in pipette

pH paper before distilled water is added

pH paper after distilled water is added

④

⑤

Magnesium oxide

CALCULATION

In this demonstration, the following measurements were recorded:

Mass of crucible and lid $= a = 35.05$ grams
Mass of crucible, lid and magnesium $= b = 36.14$ grams
Therefore, by subtraction, the mass of magnesium (Mg) $= (b - a)\ 1.09$ grams
Mass of crucible, lid and magnesium oxide $= d = 36.87$ grams
Therefore, by subtraction, the mass of oxygen (O) $= (d - b) = 0.73$ grams

From these measurements, we know that 0.73 grams of oxygen combined with 1.09 grams of magnesium to form the magnesium oxide. But, to find the number of atoms of each element in the magnesium oxide, we need to calculate the number of MOLES of the elements present.

One mole of any element contains exactly the same number of particles (atoms). The mass of a mole of an element is equal to its RELATIVE ATOMIC MASS. This can be found from a standard Periodic Table. 1 mole of magnesium has a mass of 24 grams, and 1 mole of oxygen has a mass of 16 grams (magnesium atoms are 1.5 times heavier than oxygen atoms).

Using the formula:
Mass (in grams) ÷ mass of 1 mole (in grams) = number of moles

We can calculate that:
1.09 grams ÷ 24 grams = 0.0454 moles of magnesium and
0.73 grams ÷ 16 grams = 0.0456 moles of oxygen
were present in the magnesium oxide in this demonstration. In this case, there was almost exactly one oxygen atom for every magnesium atom. The formula for magnesium oxide is therefore MgO.

MIXTURES

A mixture is a combination of two or more elements or compounds that have not reacted chemically to form new compounds. The elements or compounds in a mixture thus keep their own chemical properties. Mixtures can always be separated by physical processes, and there is no restriction on the proportions in which substances are mixed.

A mixture is different from a compound (see page 8). In a compound, the elements have joined during a chemical reaction and so are always found in fixed proportions. Not all the component elements in a compound can be separated by physical means, only through chemical reactions.

Types of mixture

Mixtures can take on many forms. If the different components are clustered in different patches, the mixture is described as heterogenous. Dry concrete, for example, is a heterogenous mixture of sand, cement and stones. Most mixtures of solids are heterogeneous mixtures.

If the components of a mixture are mixed evenly, the mixture is described as homogeneous.

For example, air is a homogeneous mixture of gases. When one substance dissolves in another to form a solution, or two gases completely mix by DIFFUSION, the individual constituents form a homogeneous mixture. For example, salt forms a homogeneous mixture when dissolved in water to form a solution. Finely divided solids such as COLLOIDS, e.g. milk, can also be homogeneous mixtures. However, when a precipitate can be seen clearly as crystals or a suspension in a solution, the mixture is heterogeneous (see page 55).

Solutions

A solution is a clear liquid mixture in which component substances *appear to be* completely blended as one. In a solution, one substance is dissolved in the other. Nevertheless, there is still no chemical reaction between the different substances.

Usually, one substance in a solution is called the SOLVENT and the second substance is called the SOLUTE. The solvent is generally the substance with the largest volume in the mixture. Gases are almost always solutes when dissolved in a liquid, which is then the solvent. Solids are commonly solutes when dissolved in liquids such as water, which are the solvents.

The way in which a liquid solute behaves depends on how it is mixed in the solvent. Some solutes mix easily in any proportion, others will only partially dissolve. In some cases, the liquid 'solute' does not dissolve but remains as very tiny droplets. In this case, it is called an EMULSION.

When solids are dissolved in liquids, they may be in the form of unchanged molecules, or they may break up into charged particles, or ions. In this

(*Right*) A 'seed' crystal of (solid) copper(II) sulphate is suspended by a thread in a solution of copper(II) sulphate. If the beaker is allowed to stand, the water will be lost to the air by evaporation, and the solution will become saturated. At this point, copper(II) sulphate solid will form on the seed crystal and it will grow to form a regular shape – rhombic. Evaporation is one way of separating a mixture.

The solution is a mixture. Because all the components are evenly distributed, the mixture is described as homogeneous.

A copper(II) sulphate solution will conduct electricity (see page 29), showing that ions are present. The crystal too is ionic (see page 8).

condition, the solution conducts electric current and is called an electrolyte.

Many chemical reactions also occur in solution, for example, the reaction between ammonium hydroxide and copper(II) sulphate solution (see page 34). Nevertheless, the solutes and solvent remain chemically separate.

The properties of solutions

Solutions are extremely important as 'vehicles' for allowing materials to be carried to where they are required to react chemically. A liquid fertiliser is an example of how a solution can be used to carry the fertiliser to the plants using a water-based solvent. All water-based solutions are called AQUEOUS SOLUTIONS and are given the abbreviation (*aq*) in chemical equations. Numerous other solutions use organic solvents such as methylbenzene.

When a substance is dissolved in a liquid, making a solution, the FREEZING POINT of the solution is lower than the freezing point of the pure liquid solvent. The most common everyday example of this is the effect of adding salt to winter roads to prevent water freezing on them. The freezing point of the salt/water solution is lower than that of pure water, so the roads are less likely to freeze over.

Separating the components of a mixture

Chemists often need to separate mixtures and obtain from them their constituent elements or compounds. A wide variety of separation techniques for gases, liquids and solids are shown on the following pages.

However, in some circumstances, chemists need to produce precisely known amounts of a mixture, usually in the form of a solution of known concentration.

Separating gases

Air, and many GASES produced during industrial processes, are mixtures. One important part of chemistry is to be able to separate out the gases so that they can be used to create useful products.

Often, one of the best ways of doing this is to lower the temperature of the gas mixture until it is a liquid – a process known as LIQUEFACTION. As the liquid mixture is heated, the individual gases can then be separated easily and collected in a process called FRACTIONAL DISTILLATION. Each gas that makes up the liquid mixture will boil off at a different temperature and can be collected. This is a common industrial method of obtaining, for example, oxygen from air.

Alternatively, it is possible to separate out a gas from a mixture of gases by binding it to a liquid or a solid. This is done, for example, using activated charcoal.

Another process is to remove a gas using a liquid solvent. Carbon dioxide, for example, is soluble in water and can be removed from air by bubbling the air through water under pressure.

Separating liquids

Liquids often occur as solutions of more than one liquid blended with another, or as liquids blended with solids. These can be separated in a number of ways.

Distillation can be used to separate liquids in much the same way as for separating gases (see above).

In the simplest kind of distillation (called simple distillation, see page 46), only the solvent vaporises, and the impurities (the solute, which does not vaporise) remain as a liquid, or may even solidify. The desalinisation of water is an example of simple distillation, where salt water is placed in a flask and boiled.

Fractional distillation is used to separate a mixture of liquids (such as crude oil) that boil at different temperatures.

In the laboratory, fractional distillation is achieved using a fractionating column and a LIEBIG CONDENSER (see page 46). The liquid mixture is heated to specific temperatures so that a range of vapours can be separated, cooled and collected as liquids called FRACTIONS.

In industry, large volumes of the separated liquids are required on a continuous basis, and so a fractionating column is used.

Steam distillation is a variant on the methods outlined above, and is used to distil liquids such as aniline that do not dissolve in water. The solution is placed in a flask with water, and steam is passed through the flask.

CHROMATOGRAPHY is a technique in which a solution is separated into its parts by passing it through a special kind of material. The various substances dissolved in the solution migrate at different speeds through the material. Sometimes they can be identified by their characteristic colours (see pages 48 to 53).

If the liquids in a mixture are IMMISCIBLE, they can be separated using a SEPARATING FUNNEL (see page 54).

Separating solids

In the laboratory, a precise separation of a mixture of solids is more difficult than for gases or liquids. It is rare that one part of the mixture can be picked out by hand or even by means of small tools. If a part of the mixture is magnetic, it is possible to separate it using a magnet (see page 55).

Solids as precipitates in solution can be removed by simple filtration (see page 56) or by using a CENTRIFUGE (see page 58). The varying abilities of the solids in a mixture to dissolve may also be exploited (see page 61).

Solids can be made to behave differently when in a SUSPENSION, so that one of the components of the mixture can be made to float for long enough for it to be skimmed off. This is the principle of the froth flotation technique (see page 62 and box on right).

In many cases, the only way of separating solids is to make them into liquids by melting, or by reacting them with liquids, such as acids, that will dissolve one or more of the solids. This is a technique called leaching.

The various temperatures at which different solids change their physical state to become liquids or gases may also be used to separate mixtures (see page 64).

SEPARATION BY FLOTATION: THE CONCENTRATION OF METAL ORES

Metals are extracted from ores. Before refining, the ore needs to be separated and concentrated. Most ore (a metal compound) contains only a small percentage of metal, so, to reduce the cost of transporting unwanted GANGUE (rock that contains no metal), the ore must be concentrated before it is sent for smelting and refining. This is done by first pulverising the ore-bearing rock to make it into a mixture of high concentration ore and gangue. This mixture is separated by flotation, and the concentrated ore dried. At the end of this process, the metal-to-ore ratio is about one to three.

The diagram below shows the process of concentration often used with copper ores, but similar processes are used with other metal ores. The ore to be enriched is first ground to a fine grit. This contains particles of copper mixed up with gangue. To separate the copper from the gangue, the grit is introduced to a bath of water containing a foaming agent, which produces a kind of bubble bath, combined with a special oil-based chemical that makes the copper particles water repellent.

When jets of air are forced up through the bath, the water-repellent copper particles are picked up by the bubbles of foam and float to the surface, making a froth. The froth is skimmed off the surface, and the enriched ore is taken away for refining.

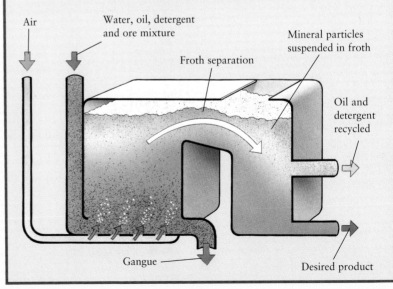

Air

Water, oil, detergent and ore mixture

Froth separation

Mineral particles suspended in froth

Oil and detergent recycled

Gangue

Desired product

Distinguishing between compounds and mixtures

Gases can occur as elements, compounds or mixtures. Here is an illustration of how to distinguish compounds from mixtures.

Demonstration 1: gases as compounds

Two gas jars are filled with different colourless gases and sealed with glass cover slips. One of the gas jars contains elemental oxygen, the other contains the compound, nitrogen monoxide. They are placed together as shown and the cover slips removed so that the gases can move freely between the two gas jars (①). Instead of creating a colourless mixture, a reaction takes place and a new brown gas (nitrogen dioxide) is formed (② & ③). The absence of oxygen from this new gas can be tested with a glowing splint, which will not rekindle.

If this new brown gas is cooled (a physical change), all of the gas liquefies and no separation occurs. A new compound has therefore been formed.

Nitrogen dioxide is a poisonous gas, and so this demonstration is performed in a fume chamber.

EQUATION: Nitrogen monoxide and oxygen
Nitrogen monoxide + oxygen ⇨ nitrogen dioxide
$2NO(g) + O_2(g) \Rightarrow 2NO_2(g)$

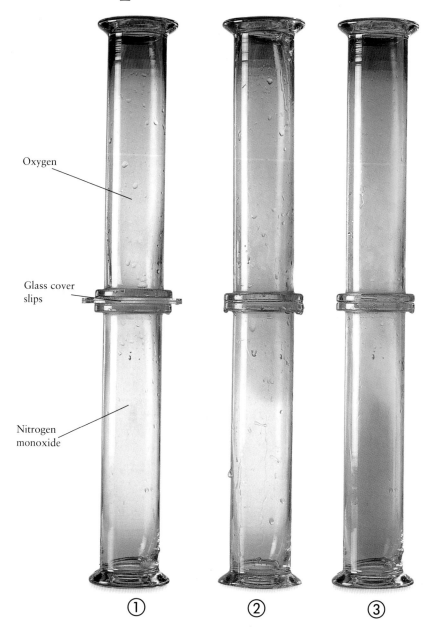

Oxygen

Glass cover slips

Nitrogen monoxide

①   ②   ③

Demonstration 2: gases as mixtures

A gas jar is filled with oxygen, which is colourless. Some drops of brown bromine liquid are added, and the gas jar sealed using a glass cover slip (④). Bromine is a poisonous gas, and so this demonstration is performed in a fume chamber.

At room temperature, the bromine liquid evaporates to give brown bromine gas. The gases now mingle freely (⑤). After some time, they mix to form a paler brown gas (⑥). If this gas is cooled, the bromine will once again become a brown liquid, leaving colourless oxygen gas above it. The oxygen can be tested for, as it will rekindle a glowing splint.

The pale brown gas is a mixture because it was separated by changing the temperature – a physical change, and no reaction has taken place.

EQUATION 1: Warming the bromine and oxygen
Bromine liquid + oxygen ⇨ bromine gas + oxygen
$Br_2(l) + O_2(g) ⇨ Br_2(g) + O_2(g)$

EQUATION 2: Cooling the bromine and oxygen
Bromine gas + oxygen ⇨ bromine liquid + oxygen
$Br_2(g) + O_2(g) ⇨ Br_2(l) + O_2(g)$

④   ⑤   ⑥

Separating liquids and solids by distillation

Simple distillation separates a solvent from a solution by making use of the boiling point of the solvent.

Demonstration: simple distillation of water

Simple distillation (①), such as the distillation of water from a salt solution, uses a flask coupled to a Liebig condenser (②). A Liebig condenser is a convenient apparatus for condensing a vapour into a liquid. It consists of a water jacket around a central delivery tube. Cold, tap water is passed through the water jacket, removing heat from the delivery tube,

and so causing the vapour in the tube to condense. The condensed liquid, known as the DISTILLATE, is collected in a separate container.

For this demonstration, common salt (sodium chloride) was dissolved in distilled water to give a

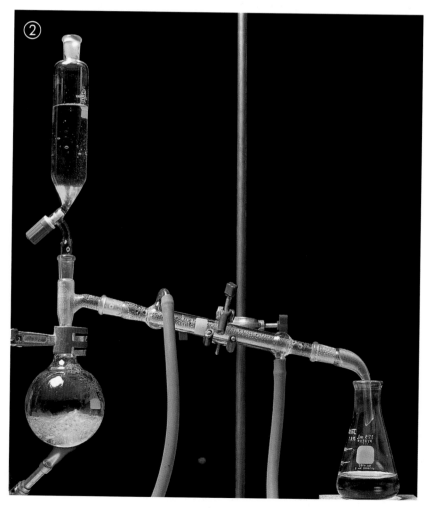

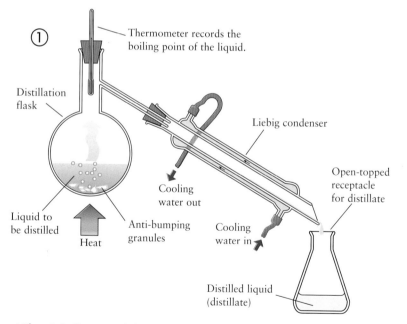

① Thermometer records the boiling point of the liquid.

Distillation flask

Liebig condenser

Cooling water out

Open-topped receptacle for distillate

Liquid to be distilled

Heat

Anti-bumping granules

Cooling water in

Distilled liquid (distillate)

(*Above*) A diagram of the apparatus used in simple distillation.
A thermometer can be used to gauge the boiling point accurately in a distillation. To boil off the water, the temperature would be kept at 100°C.

colourless aqueous solution of sodium chloride. A dye was added to give the solution its yellow colour and to show the separation. In this case, a dropper funnel has been attached to the distillation flask so that the salt solution can be added gradually during heating. The picture ((3)) shows how a thermometer might be used.

Some inert ANTI-BUMPING GRANULES are added to the distillation flask, and some sodium chloride solution is dripped in. The solution is then heated until it boils. The anti-bumping granules ensure smooth boiling without excessive formation of large bubbles. The vapour which is pure, distilled water without any dye, passes through the Liebig condenser, cools and condenses to a liquid, and is collected in the conical flask. The sodium chloride and the dye in the mixture are left behind in the distillation flask. The solution will become more concentrated and, if boiled dry, the salt and dye would be left behind as solids.

Remarks

Distillation can be used for separating mixtures of a number of liquids. This is called fractional distillation. To achieve fractional separation, a thermometer and a fractionating column are required. The heating can then be adjusted to just above the BOILING POINT of each individual component of the mixture in turn, and the distillate collected at each stage.

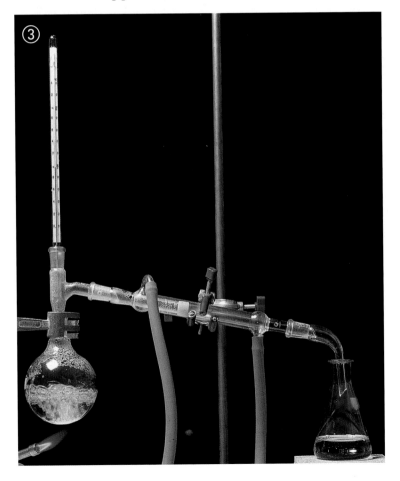

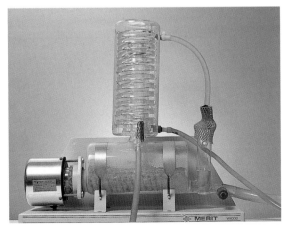

(*Right*) The laboratory production of distilled water uses simple distillation. Pure water is evaporated from tap water, which contains many solid impurities.

Separating the components of a liquid mixture using thin-layer chromatography

Chromatography is a method of separating the components of a solution. It works because different solutes in a solution have varying abilities to dissolve in the solvent.

In chromatography, the solution is passed through an appropriate substance, such as a sheet or column (see page 52), and the different solid components (solutes) are ADSORBED on to the surface of that substance at different rates.

Thin-layer chromatography uses a sheet of solid, e.g. aluminium oxide.

Note that thin-layer chromatography is more a method for identifying the parts of a solution than a method for separating the substances for collection.

Demonstration 1: thin-layer chromatography using aluminium oxide sheet

In thin-layer chromatography, an aluminium sheet can be used, coated in a thin layer of a mixture of aluminium oxide, which is held in place with a binder.

A line is drawn with a pencil across the lower part of the sheet. This acts as a reference line. Small amounts of the solution under investigation, together with small amounts of the likely pure components, are placed as spots along the pencil line.

The sheet is now ready to be placed in a chromatography tank. In the bottom of the tank is a shallow depth of some suitable solvent, in this case alcohol.

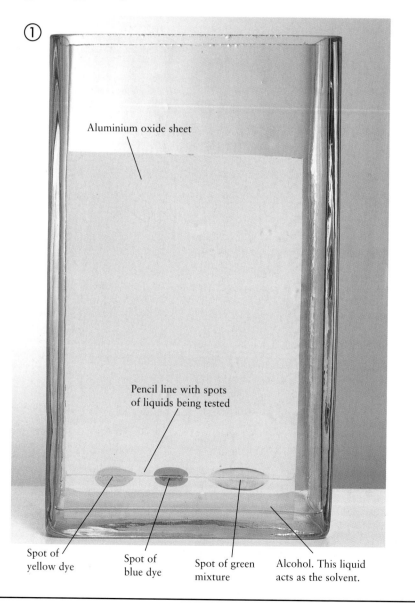

① Aluminium oxide sheet

Pencil line with spots of liquids being tested

Spot of yellow dye

Spot of blue dye

Spot of green mixture

Alcohol. This liquid acts as the solvent.

The chromatography sheet is placed so that the bottom of it dips into the solvent (①). The surface of the alcohol is below the pencil line and the spotted samples. A lid is now be placed on the tank so that the atmosphere inside the tank is saturated with solvent. This prevents the sheet from drying out.

Over the next few minutes, the solvent begins to soak up like blotting paper into the sheet by CAPILLARY action. As soon as it reaches the spots of test mixture, it dissolves them and begins to wash each component upwards.

In this demonstration, a yellow and blue dye have been mixed together to create a green test substance. This is spotted on the reference line. Pure yellow dye and blue dye are also spotted along the same line. As there are yellow and blue in the green mixture, the blue component of the mixture flows up the sheet to the same level as the pure blue substance, and the yellow component of the mixture flows up the sheet to the same level as the yellow dye. The resulting sheet with the separations is called a chromatogram (②).

Remarks

Aluminium oxide is commonly used for chromatography. However, alternative media, such as microcellulose, can be used. The important property of any chromatography material is that it allows liquids to be adsorbed on the surface of the medium without sticking so hard that they cannot move.

Greater sensitivity for a particular purpose can be achieved by changing the solvent or the surface properties of the aluminium oxide. For example, the surface of the aluminium oxide can be deactivated slightly by applying dilute acetic acid.

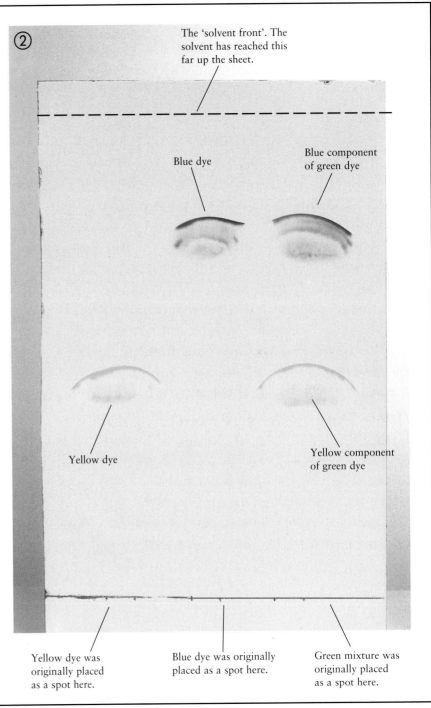

② The 'solvent front'. The solvent has reached this far up the sheet.

Blue dye

Blue component of green dye

Yellow dye

Yellow component of green dye

Yellow dye was originally placed as a spot here.

Blue dye was originally placed as a spot here.

Green mixture was originally placed as a spot here.

Demonstration 2: paper chromatography using single grain paper

Paper chromatography is similar in principle to thin-layer sheet chromatography but uses paper, which is less expensive.

In this case, the demonstration will attempt to find out whether three apparently identical chemical indicator solutions, supplied by three different chemical companies, do indeed contain the same substances.

Three samples of indicator are spotted along the pencil line. In this case the solvent trough (filled with alcohol) is suspended near the top of the chromatography trough. The end of the paper is dipped in the alcohol and held in place by a glass rod. The remainder of the paper is allowed to hang down in the trough, and a lid placed on the tank (③ & ④).

The alcohol soaks into the paper and then flows down the paper sheet under gravity (⑤). In this case, the yellow component of the mixture is rather more soluble in the alcohol than the red and so flows slightly faster, giving a colour separation. However, in all other respects the pattern of separation is the same, indicating that the three samples contain the same mixture.

Remarks

The paper used for paper chromatography has a grain which runs in straight lines and thus directs the spread of the components of the mixture into parallel lines.

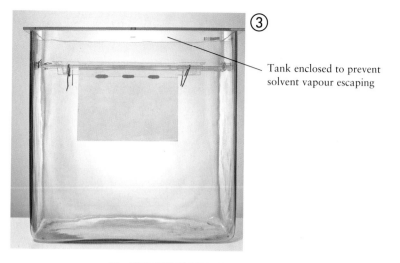

③

Tank enclosed to prevent solvent vapour escaping

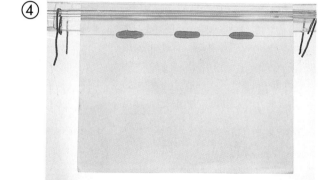

④

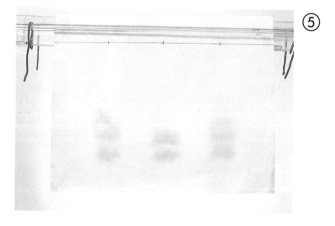

⑤

Demonstration 3: paper chromatography using filter paper

This demonstration shows the effect of using filter paper when a chromatography tank is not available. In this case, felt-tipped pen ink is being tested. Coloured inks contain many dyes.

The filter paper is formed into a cone and then some spots of ink are placed along a line (⑥). These are water-soluble dyes, and so the filter paper is placed in a dish of water. The colours of the components of the ink can be seen clearly (⑦ & ⑧).

⑧

⑥

Filter paper folded to make a cone

Dish containing water

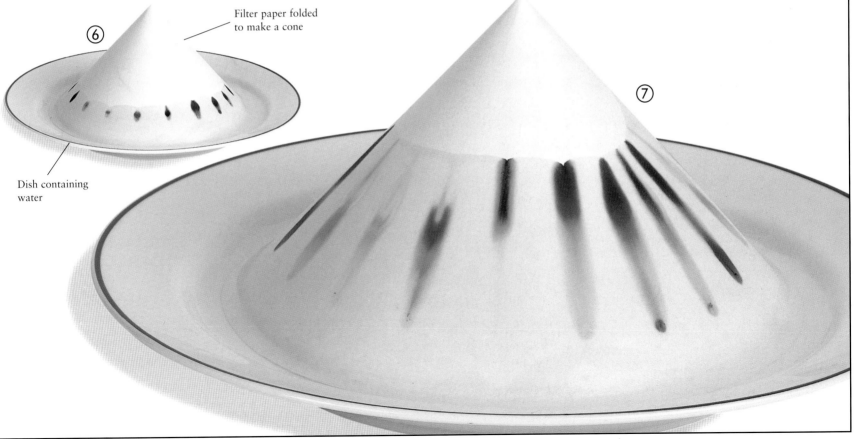

⑦

Separating a mixture using column chromatography

① Pestle and mortar

Chromatography does not have to be performed using a sheet, but can also be performed using a column of non-reactive material. In this case, samples of the different fractions can be collected for further use. In this demonstration, the separating column contains aluminium oxide (as was used on the sheet in the demonstration on page 48), and the solution under test contains red vegetable dyes, extracted from beetroots.

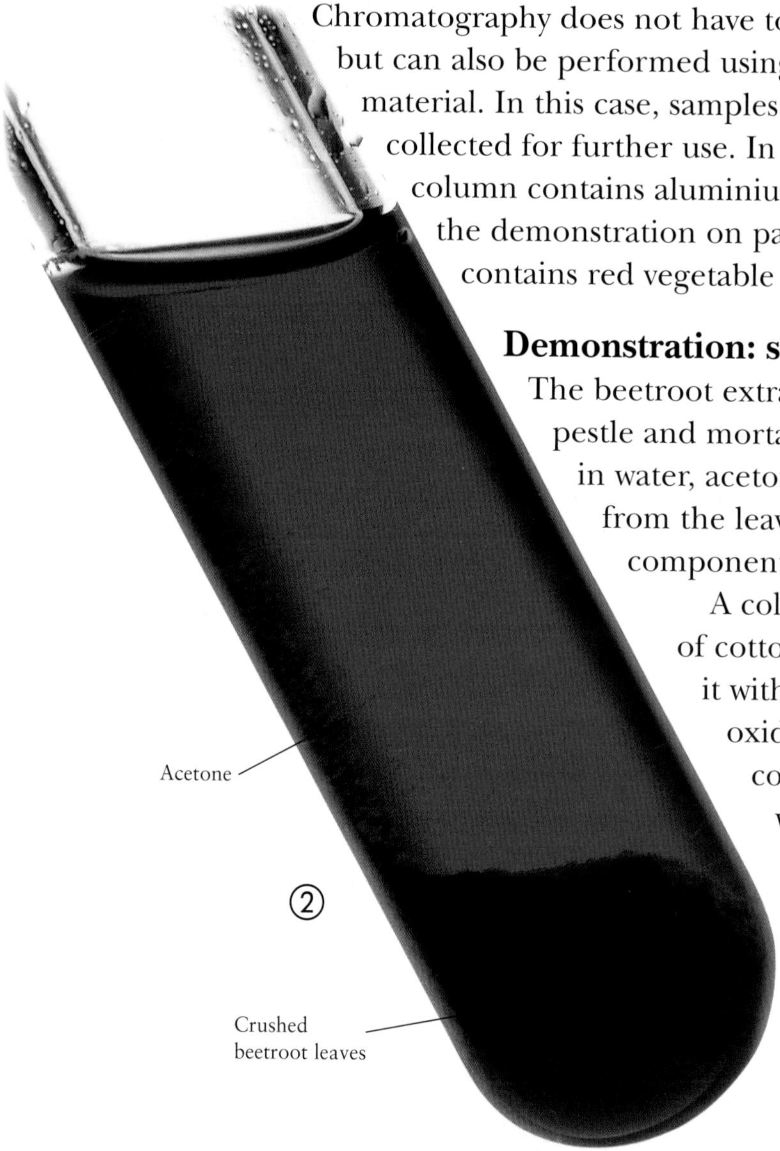

Demonstration: separation of beetroot extract

The beetroot extract is first prepared by crushing raw beetroot using a pestle and mortar (①). In this case, although beetroot juice dissolves in water, acetone is used (②) because it extracts the colouring matter from the leaves and stems and allows a good separation of the components in the separating column.

A column of aluminium oxide is prepared by pushing a wad of cotton wool into one end of a long, glass tube and then filling it with acetone. The cotton wool will hold the aluminium oxide, while allowing liquids to pass through. A separating column could be used; the column contains a porous disc which will perform the same task as the cotton wool.

Aluminium oxide is now added slowly so that the column fills with a mixture that has an even texture (③). This will be the chromatography 'STATIONARY PHASE' (see page 53), causing the components of the juice to move at different speeds.

Acetone

② Crushed beetroot leaves

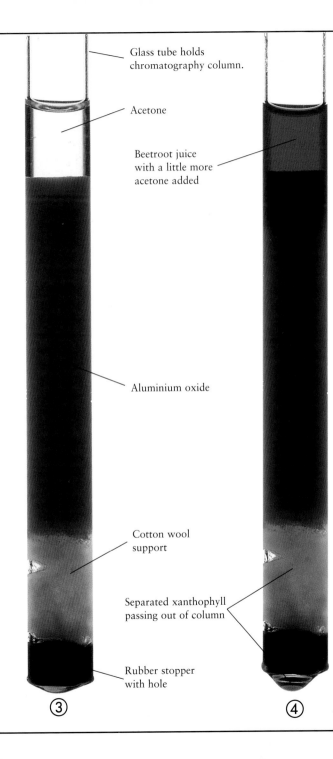

Glass tube holds
chromatography column.

Acetone

Beetroot juice
with a little more
acetone added

Aluminium oxide

Cotton wool
support

Separated xanthophyll
passing out of column

Rubber stopper
with hole

③

④

The juice is next poured on the top of the column, and more acetone added to wash it right through (③). Within a few moments, colour separations can be seen down the tube as the various components of the mixture separate out (④).

It takes about five minutes for the first component of the beetroot juice to drip from the base of the tube. It is a yellow substance (xanthophyll) (⑤). After a few minutes more, the colour of the liquid begins to change. When it is collected, it is found to be a green substance, in this case, chlorophyll (the green pigment in plants) (⑥).

Remarks

A substance like aluminium oxide, used in this way, is called a stationary phase. Substances easily attach to its surface (a process called adsorption) and are also easily washed off again. Each substance sticks to the aluminium oxide to a different degree, so that the least firmly stuck can be washed off most easily, and so on. As a result, the various compounds making up the original substance wash out of the base of the column one at a time, and can be collected separately.

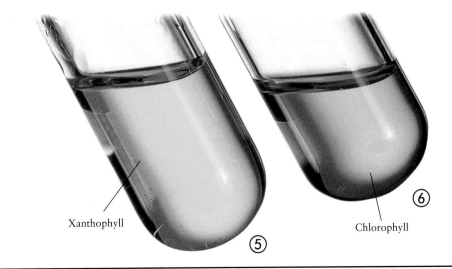

Xanthophyll

⑤

Chlorophyll

⑥

Separating immiscible liquids using a separating funnel

A separating funnel is a piece of apparatus designed to allow easy separation of two liquids that are IMMISCIBLE – that is they do not mix. The easiest way to separate two immiscible liquids is to drain off the more dense liquid first.

The key to successful separation is therefore to ensure that there is an accurate way of draining the denser liquid without any drops of the less dense liquid contaminating it. This is the purpose of the tear-drop shape of the separating funnel, where, towards the tap, the cross-sectional area is progressively smaller. This means that, while a large amount of liquid can be held in the funnel, the narrowing neck makes it easier to see when all of the more dense liquid has been drained off.

Demonstration: separating an aqueous solution of potassium permanganate from carbon tetrachloride

In this demonstration, a purple potassium permanganate solution is to be separated from colourless carbon tetrachloride. The two liquids are poured into the separating funnel (①). The clear carbon tetrachloride is more dense than the potassium permanganate solution and so it sinks to the bottom of the funnel.

The tap is opened and the carbon tetrachloride is run out into a beaker (②). When almost all of the carbon tetrachloride has flowed out, the tap is partly closed. This slows down the rate at which liquid flows through the tap.

As the last few drops of carbon tetrachloride are run out, the glass tap is studied closely. The advantage of the glass tap is that you can see the liquid inside it. The objective is to close the tap fully when the last of the carbon tetrachloride is leaving the tap, and the potassium permanganate solution is just entering it (③).

Once the carbon tetrachloride has been separated (④), it can be taken away and the tap opened partially to allow the small residual amount trapped in the tube to be flushed out by the incoming potassium permanganate solution. Once the flushing process is complete, the tap can be opened wide and the rest of the potassium permanganate solution poured into a separate beaker. Alternatively, the solution could simply be poured out of the top of the funnel.

Remarks

These particular liquids were chosen so that the demonstration can be seen clearly. There are many occasions where chemists use this technique to separate a solution in water from a solution in an organic solvent (such as ether or carbon tetrachloride) as part of the purification of a product.

Separation of a mixture of solids by magnetism

A mixture containing magnetic and non-magnetic materials can be separated using magnetism.

Demonstration: separating iron from sulphur

Iron and sulphur form distinctively coloured powders (see page 15). When iron filings and sulphur are mixed, the dark brown iron can be seen speckling the yellow sulphur (①). This is a heterogeneous mixture.

When a magnet is placed in the mixture and moved about, the iron filings attach themselves to it, and can be drawn away from the sulphur (②). Contrast this with a compound of iron and sulphur called iron(II) sulphide shown on page 16.

Iron filings separated using a bar magnet

Heterogenous mixture of iron filings and sulphur powder

Separating a precipitate from a solution using filtration

FILTRATION is one of the most fundamental techniques for separating mixtures of solids and liquids.

Demonstration: filtering lead iodide

A simple filtration uses a conical flask, a funnel and a disc of filter paper (①). The filter paper is folded twice and opened in such a way as to fit into the funnel (②). The paper is then wetted with distilled water to make it sit firmly in the funnel.

In this demonstration, a precipitate of yellow lead iodide is to be separated from a solution contained in a boiling tube. To make sure the entire mixture goes into the funnel, the contents are swirled in the boiling tube and then poured boldly into the funnel (③). A glass rod is used to guide the liquid on to the filter paper without splashing, and gravity carries the liquid through to the flask below.

A jet of distilled water, squirted from a wash bottle, is used to wash all solution from the funnel and into the flask (④). The solution in the flask is called the FILTRATE. The particles of PRECIPITATE are too large to pass through the filter paper and are held on the surface as a yellow deposit (called the 'residue').

The filter paper is then removed from the funnel, opened out with the precipitate upwards, and left to stand in a dust-free place until it is dried. The

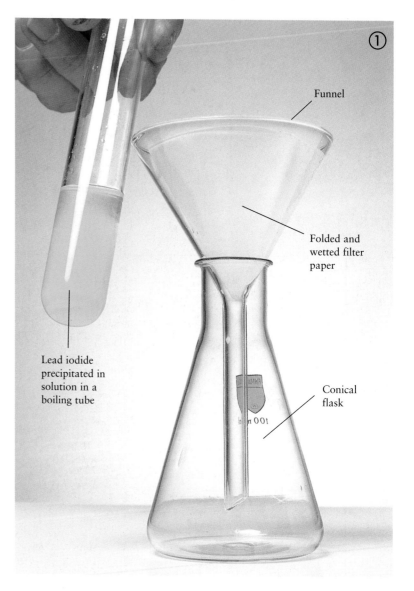

Funnel

Folded and wetted filter paper

Lead iodide precipitated in solution in a boiling tube

Conical flask

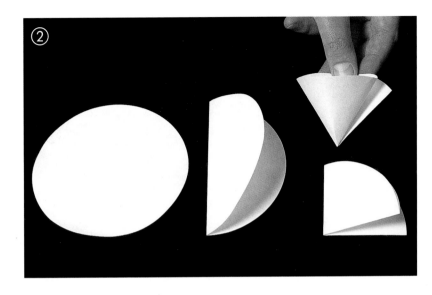

precipitate can now be removed and collected from the filter paper (③). First, the paper is flexed to break the deposit away from the paper surface and then the paper is tapped gently to shake off the deposit.

Remarks

Notice that it is important to get all of the precipitate from the boiling tube in which it was first prepared. The washing stage is also very important for any quantitative technique. Note also that some solutions will not be soluble in water and so, in such cases, an alternative 'washing' liquid may have to be used. Under no circumstances should the dried precipitate be scraped off the filter paper because this will also scrape off some cellulose paper fibres and contaminate the sample of filtered solid.

Conical flask

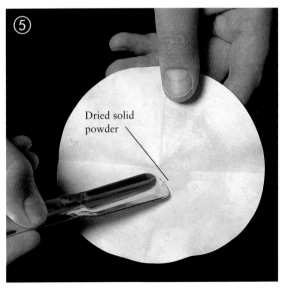

Distilled water

Wash bottle

Filtrate in dilute solution

Dried solid powder

Separating a precipitate from a solution using a centrifuge

One common result of a chemical reaction is to produce a precipitate and a solution. The precipitate can be filtered off as described on page 57, or it can be centrifuged, as shown here.

Demonstration: centrifuging a precipitate of copper(I) iodide

In this demonstration, we first create a precipitate by reacting two liquids. The precipitate is then separated from the solution by centrifuging. If a colourless solution of potassium iodide is added to a beaker containing copper(II) sulphate solution (①),

iodine is liberated, which turns the solution brown (②). This shows that the iodide ion has been oxidised to iodine.

The copper(II) ions are reduced and produce a white precipitate of copper(I) iodide, which is formed throughout the solution as tiny white particles called a suspension. These make the solution appear cloudy, and a combination of the white precipitate with the brown iodine make the resultant solution appear like a chocolate milk-shake (③)!

EQUATION: Producing a copper(I) iodide precipitate
Potassium iodide + copper(II) sulphate ⇨ copper(I) iodide + iodine + potassium sulphate

$$4KI(aq) + 2CuSO_4(aq) \Rightarrow 2CuI(s) + I_2(aq) + 2K_2SO_4(aq)$$
White

①

Pipette loaded with potassium iodide

Copper(II) sulphate solution

②

③

Copper(I) iodide suspension

To obtain a pure sample of the copper(I) iodide precipitate, a centrifuge is used.

First a sample of the liquid mixture is poured into a tube (④) and this is placed in a holder in the centrifuge. The centrifuge is started and, as it spins (⑤), the more dense precipitate is thrown to the end of the tube, leaving a clear brown solution above (⑥).

After the first spin, most of the solution in the tube is decanted (taken off) using a pipette. A little distilled water is then added to the tube. The SEDIMENT is then shaken up with the water and centrifuged again. This process is equivalent to washing the precipitate through a filter paper (see page 57), and is repeated until all the brown solution has been removed. At this stage, the tube contains only distilled water above a sediment of white copper(I) iodide (⑦). The solid can now be dried to complete the separation.

Remarks

Centrifuging techniques are best suited to small samples, rather than to large quantities of material. When a centrifuge is operating, the lid must always be closed.

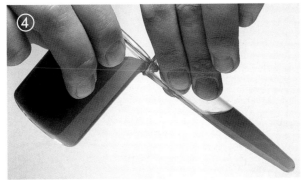

(Above) The centrifuge must be balanced to spin evenly. For every tube placed in the centrifuge, one of similar weight must be placed in an opposite holder.

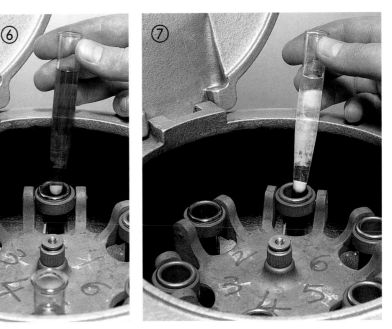

Separating mixtures of solids by solution

Many mixtures are difficult to separate as solids. This demonstration shows how it can be achieved if one of the solids will dissolve.

Demonstration: separating a mixture of copper(II) sulphate and cadmium sulphide

A mixture of blue copper(II) sulphate crystals and yellow cadmium sulphide crystals is difficult to separate (①). However, if distilled water is added to the mixture (②), the copper(II) sulphate will dissolve (③). The mixture is washed into a beaker. The cadmium sulphide crystals are insoluble and remain as a precipitate.

However, simply washing the copper sulphate from the watch glass leaves a contaminated residue on the cadmium sulphide (④). So, to separate the two substances completely, the mixture is filtered using a funnel and filter paper (⑤), following the method shown on page 57. The solution can be washed more thoroughly using distilled water. The bright yellow

①

②

Watch glass

Wash bottle containing distilled water

③

Copper(II) sulphate solution

However, there are still considerable quantities of sulphide mixed in the bottom sediment. To move these, a thin glass tube is used to blow air through the sediment and give the bubbles a chance to help pull the sulphide clear of the sand (⑥).

The scum of concentrated oily copper sulphide can then be scraped off the surface using a piece of filter paper (⑦).

Remarks

This demonstration shows the principle of flotation. In the commercial operation, a complex wetting and frothing agent is used, together with constant stirring and powerful jets of air (see page 43). These are far more effective than washing-up detergent and light machine oil.

⑥ Air blown through a glass tube

⑦ Shovel-shaped piece of filter paper

⑤

Separation of a mixture of solids by sublimation

When most solids are heated sufficiently, they will change physical state, or phase, to a liquid and then to a gas. Some solids can change state directly to a gas, in which case they are said to sublime.

Different solids change their physical state at different temperatures. If the solids in a mixture change phase at very different temperatures, this property may be used to separate them.

Demonstration: separating salt and iodine

Common salt (sodium chloride) and iodine can exist as solids at room temperature. However, iodine sublimes on gentle heating, whereas salt only melts to its LIQUID PHASE on extreme heating. Thus the two substances can be separated readily.

A mixture of iodine and salt crystals is tipped into the bottom of a conical flask. Iodine vapour is poisonous and so the entire demonstration is performed in a fume chamber.

The mixture is gently heated and the solid iodine quickly sublimes to a purple vapour, which then fills the conical flask (①).

Hot iodine vapour occupies more space than the solid from which it has sublimed, so it is not sensible to seal the conical flask. Instead, a ceramic disc is used as a cover slip. As pressure builds up in the flask, the disc will lift slightly until the pressure falls. Thus, a little hot vapour will escape, but the minimum possible amount of iodine will be lost.

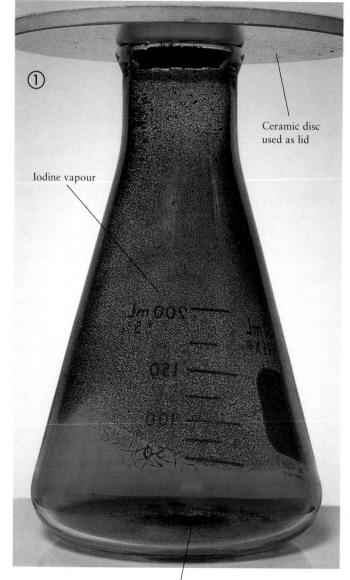

① Ceramic disc used as lid

Iodine vapour

Mixture of salt and iodine crystals is placed in bottom of conical flask.

The iodine vapour soon begins to change back to a solid phase and form a deposit of small crystals on the cool, upper part of the conical flask (②). Once a few crystals have begun to form, they act as centres of growth, and more solid is deposited on to them (③). The salt is left behind in the bottom of the flask (④).

Remarks

If all the iodine has to be collected without loss, the vapour should be led off to a separate container where it can sublime to form a deposit and be collected. This is a form of distillation.

④

Iodine crystal deposits on glass surface.

②

Iodine crystal deposits on glass surface.

③

Salt crystals are left behind.

NOTE: Ice can be made to sublime at reduced pressure. The water vapour that is produced is used in the manufacture of dried food and instant coffee granules in a process known as 'freeze drying'.

MASTER GLOSSARY

absolute zero: the lowest possible temperature ($-273.15°C$).

absorption: the process by which a substance is soaked up. *See:* adsorption.

acid: a substance that can give a proton to another substance. Acids are compounds, containing hydrogen, that can attack and dissolve many substances. Acids are described as weak or strong, dilute or concentrated, mineral or organic. *Example:* hydrochloric acid (HCl). An acid in water can react with a base to form a salt and water.

acidic solution: a solution with a pH lower than 7.

acidity: a general term for the strength of an acid in a solution.

acid radical: the negative ion left behind when an acid loses a hydrogen ion. *Example:* Cl⁻ in hydrochloric acid (HCl).

acid salt: An ACID SALT contains at least one hydrogen ion and can behave as an acid in chemical reactions. Acid salts are produced under conditions that do not allow complete neutralisation of the acid. For example, sulphuric acid may react with a sodium compound to produce a normal sodium salt, sodium sulphate (Na_2SO_4), or it may retain some of the hydrogen, in which case it becomes the salt sodium hydrogen sulphate ($NaHSO_4$).

actinide series or actinide metals: a series of 15 similar radioactive elements between actinium and lawrencium. They are transition metals.

activated charcoal: a form of carbon, made up of tiny crystals of graphite, which is made by heating organic matter in the absence of air. It is then processed further to increase its pore space and therefore its surface area. Its surface area is about $2000\ m^2/g$. Activated charcoal readily adsorbs many gases and it is therefore widely used as a filter, for example, in gas masks.

activation energy: the energy required to make a reaction occur. The greater the activation energy of a reaction, the more its reaction rate depends on temperature. The activation energy of a reaction is useful because, if the rate of reaction is known at one temperature (for example, 100 °C) then the activation energy can be used to calculate the rate of reaction at another temperature (for example, 400 °C) without actually doing the experiment.

adsorption: the process by which a surface adsorbs a substance. The substances involved are not chemically combined and can be separated. *Example:* the adsorption properties of activated charcoal. *See:* absorption.

alchemy: the traditional 'art' of working with chemicals that prevailed through the Middle Ages. One of the main challenges for alchemists was to make gold from lead. Alchemy faded away as scientific chemistry was developed in the 17th century.

alcohol: an organic compound which contains a hydroxyl (OH) group. *Example:* ethanol (CH_3CH_2OH), also known as ethyl alcohol or grain alcohol.

alkali/alkaline: a base in (aqueous) solution. Alkalis react with, or neutralise, hydrogen ions in acids and have a pH greater than 7.0 because they contain relatively few hydrogen ions. *Example:* aqueous sodium hydroxide (NaOH).

alkaline cell (or battery): a dry cell in which the electrolyte contains sodium or potassium hydroxide.

alkaline earth metal: a member of Group 2 of the Periodic Table. *Example:* calcium.

alkali metals: a member of Group 1 of the Periodic Table. *Example:* sodium.

alkane: a hydrocarbon with no carbon-to-carbon multiple bonds. *Example:* ethane, C_2H_6.

alkene: a hydrocarbon with at least one carbon-to-carbon double bond. *Example:* ethene, C_2H_4.

alkyne: a hydrocarbon with at least one carbon-to-carbon triple bond. *Example:* ethyne, C_2H_2.

allotropes: alternative forms of an element that differ in the way the atoms are linked. *Example:* white and red phosphorus.

alloy: a mixture of a metal and various other elements. *Example:* brass is an alloy of copper and zinc.

amalgam: a liquid alloy of mercury with another metal.

amorphous: a solid in which the atoms are not arranged regularly (i.e. glassy). Compare crystalline.

amphoteric: a metal that will react with both acids and alkalis. *Example:* aluminium metal.

anhydrous: lacking water; water has been removed, for example, by heating. Many hydrated salts are crystalline. (Opposite of anhydrous is hydrous or hydrated.) *Example:* copper(II) sulphate can be anhydrous ($CuSO_4$) or hydrated ($CuSO_4 \bullet 5H_2O$).

anion: a negatively charged atom or group of atoms. *Examples:* chloride ion (Cl⁻), hydroxide ion (OH⁻).

anode: the electrode at which oxidation occurs; the negative terminal of a battery or the positive electrode of an electrolysis cell.

anodising: a process that uses the effect of electrolysis to make a surface corrosion resistant. *Example:* anodised aluminium.

antacid: a common name for any compound that reacts with stomach acid to neutralise it. *Example:* sodium hydrogen carbonate, also known as sodium bicarbonate.

antioxidant: a substance that reacts rapidly with radicals thereby preventing oxidation of some other substance.

anti-bumping granules: small glass or ceramic beads, designed to promote boiling without the development of large gas bubbles.

approximate relative atomic mass: *See:* relative atomic mass.

aqueous: a solution in which the solvent is water. Usually used as 'aqueous solution'. *Example:* aqueous solution of sodium hydroxide (NaOH(aq)).

aromatic hydrocarbons: compounds of carbon that have the benzene ring as part of their structure. *Examples:* benzene (C_6H_6), naphthalene ($C_{10}H_8$). They are known as aromatic because of the strong pungent smell given off by benzene.

atmospheric pressure: the pressure exerted by the gases in the air. Units of measurement are kilopascals (kPa), atmospheres (atm), millimetres of mercury (mm Hg) and Torr. Standard atmospheric pressure is 100 kPa, 1atm, 760 mm Hg or 760 Torr.

atom: the smallest particle of an element; a nucleus and its surrounding electrons.

atomic mass: the mass of an atom measured in atomic mass units (amu). An atomic mass unit is equal to one-twelfth of the atom of carbon-12. Atomic mass is now more generally used instead of atomic weight. *Example:* the atomic mass of chlorine is about 35 amu. *See:* atomic weight, relative atomic mass.

atomic number: also known as proton number. The number of electrons or the number of protons in an atom. *Example:* the atomic number of gold is 79 and for carbon it is 4.

atomic structure: the nucleus and the arrangement of electrons around the nucleus of an atom.

atomic weight: a common term used to mean the average molar mass of an element. This is the mass per mole of atoms. *Example:* the atomic weight of chlorine is about 35 g/mol. *See:* atomic mass, mole.

base: a substance that can accept a proton from another substance. *Example:* aqueous ammonia ($NH_3(aq)$). A base can react with an acid in water to form a salt and water.

basic salt: a salt that contains at least one hydroxide ion. The hydroxide ion can then behave as a base in chemical reactions. *Example:* the reaction of hydrochloric acid (HCl) with the base, aluminium hydroxide ($Al(OH)_3$) can form two basic salts, $Al(OH)_2Cl$ and $Al(OH)Cl_2$.

battery: a number of electrochemical cells placed in series.

bauxite: a hydrated impure oxide of aluminium ($Al_2O_3 \bullet xH_2O$, with the amount of water x being variable). It is the main ore used to obtain aluminium metal. The reddish-brown colour of bauxite is mainly caused by the iron oxide impurities it contains.

beehive shelf: an inverted earthenware bowl with a hole in the upper surface and a slot in the rim. Traditionally, the earthenware was brown and looked similar to a beehive, hence its name. A delivery tube passes through the slot and a gas jar is placed over the hole. This provides a convenient way to collect gas over water in a pneumatic trough.

bell jar: a tall glass jar with an open bottom and a wide, stoppered neck that is used in conjunction with a beehive shelf and a pneumatic trough in some experiments involving gases. The name derives from historic versions of the apparatus, which resembled a bell in shape.

blast furnace: a tall furnace charged with a mixture of iron ore, coke and limestone and used for the refining of iron metal. The name comes from the strong blast of air introduced during smelting.

bleach: a substance that removes colour in stains on materials, either by oxidising or reducing the staining compound. *Example:* sulphur dioxide (SO_2).

block: one of the main divisions of the Periodic Table. Blocks are named for the outermost, occupied electron shell of an element. *Example:* The Transition Metals all belong to the d-block.

boiling point: the temperature at which a liquid boils, changing from a liquid to a gas. Boiling points change with atmospheric pressure. *Example:* The boiling point of pure water at standard atmospheric pressure is 100 °C.

boiling tube: A thin glass tube closed at one end and used for chemical tests, etc. The composition and thickness of the glass is such that it cannot sustain very high temperatures and is intended for heating liquids to boiling point. *See:* side-arm boiling tube, test tube.

bond: chemical bonding is either a transfer or sharing of electrons by two or more atoms. There are a number of types of chemical bond, some very strong (such as covalent and ionic bonds), others weak (such as hydrogen bonds). Chemical bonds form because the linked molecule is more stable than the unlinked atoms from which it formed. *Example:* the hydrogen molecule (H_2) is more stable than single atoms of hydrogen, which is why hydrogen gas is always found as molecules of two hydrogen atoms.

Boyle's Law: At constant temperature, and for a given mass of gas, the volume of the gas (V) is inversely proportional to pressure that builds up (P): $P \propto 1/V$.

brine: a solution of salt (sodium chloride, NaCl) in water.

Büchner flask: a thick-walled side-arm flask designed to withstand the changes in pressure that occur when the flask is connected to a suction pump.

Büchner funnel: a special design of plastic or ceramic funnel which has a flat stage on which a filter paper can be placed. It is intended for use under suction with a Büchner funnel.

buffer (solution): a mixture of substances in solution that resists a change in the acidity or alkalinity of the solution when small amounts of an acid or alkali are added.

burette: a long, graduated glass tube with a tap at one end. A burette is used vertically, with the tap lowermost. Its main use is as a reservoir for a chemical during titration.

burn: a combustion reaction in which a flame is produced. A flame occurs where *gases* combust and release heat and light. At least two gases are therefore required if there is to be a flame. *Example:* methane gas (CH_4) burns in oxygen gas (O_2) to produce carbon dioxide (CO_2) and water (H_2O) and give out heat and light.

calorimeter: an insulated container designed to prevent heat gain or loss with the environment and thus allow changes of temperature within reacting chemicals to be measured accurately. It is named after the old unit of heat, the calorie.

capillary: a very small diameter (glass) tube. Capillary tubing has a small enough diameter to allow surface tension effects to retain water within the tube.

capillary action: the tendency for a liquid to be sucked into small spaces, such as between objects and through narrow-pore tubes. The force to do this comes from surface tension.

carbohydrate: a compound containing only carbon, hydrogen and oxygen. Carbohydrates have the formula $C_n(H_2O)_n$, where n is variable. *Example:* glucose ($C_6H_{12}O_6$).

carbonate: a salt of carbonic acid. Carbonate ions have the chemical formula CO_3^{2-}. *Examples:* calcium nitrate $CaCO_3$ and sodium carbonate Na_2CO_3.

catalyst: a substance that speeds up a chemical reaction, but itself remains unaltered at the end of the reaction. *Example:* copper in the reaction of hydrochloric acid with zinc.

catalytic converter: a device incorporated into some exhaust systems. The catalytic converter contains a framework and/or granules with a very large surface area and coated with catalysts that convert the pollutant gases passing over them into harmless products.

cathode: the electrode at which reduction occurs; the positive terminal of a battery or the negative electrode of an electrolysis cell.

cathodic protection: the technique of protecting a metal object by connecting it to a more readily oxidisable metal. The metal object being protected is made into the cathode of a cell. *Example:* iron can be protected by coupling it with magnesium. Iron forms the cathode and magnesium the anode.

cation: a positively charged ion. *Examples:* calcium ion (Ca^{2+}), ammonium ion (NH_4^+).

caustic: a substance that can cause burns if it touches the skin. *Example:* Sodium hydroxide, caustic soda (NaOH).

Celsius scale (°C): a temperature scale on which the freezing point of water is at 0 degrees and the normal boiling point at standard atmospheric pressure is 100 degrees.

cell: a vessel containing two electrodes and an electrolyte that can act as an electrical conductor.

centrifuge: an instrument for spinning small samples very rapidly. The fast spin causes the components of a mixture that have a different density to separate. This has the same effect as filtration.

ceramic: a material based on clay minerals which has been heated so that it has chemically hardened.

chalcogens: the members of Group 6 of the Periodic Table: oxygen, sulphur, selenium and tellurium. The word comes from the Greek meaning 'brass giver', because all these elements are found in copper ores, and copper is the most important metal in making brass.

change of state: a change between two of the three states of matter, solid, liquid and gas. *Example:* when water evaporates it changes from a liquid to a gaseous state.

Charles's Law: The volume (V) of a given mass of gas at constant pressure is directly proportional to its absolute temperature (T): $V \propto T$.

chromatography: A separation technique uses the ability of surfaces to adsorb substances with different strengths. The substances with the least adherence to the surface move faster and leave behind those that adhere more strongly.

coagulation: a term describing the tendency of small particles to stick together in clumps.

coherent: meaning that a substance holds together or sticks together well, and without holes or other defects. *Example:* Aluminium appears unreactive because, as soon as new metal is exposed to air, it forms a very complete oxide coating, which then stops further reaction occurring.

coinage metals: the elements copper, silver and gold, used to make coins.

coke: a solid substance left after the gases have been extracted from coal.

colloid: a mixture of ultramicroscopic particles dispersed uniformly through a second substance to form a suspension which may be almost like a solution or may set to a jelly (gel). The word comes from the Greek for glue.

colorimeter: an instrument for measuring the light-absorbing power of a substance. The absorption gives an accurate indication of the concentration of some coloured solutions.

combustion: a reaction in which an element or compound is oxidised to release energy. Some combustion reactions are slow, such as the combustion of the sugar we eat to provide our energy. If the combustion results in a flame, it is called burning. A flame occurs where *gases* combust and release heat and light. At least two gases are therefore required if there is to be a flame. *Example:* the combustion or burning of methane gas (CH_4) in oxygen gas (O_2) produces carbon dioxide (CO_2) and water (H_2O) and gives out heat and light. Some combustion reactions produce light and heat but do not produce flames. *Example:* the combustion of carbon in oxygen produces an intense red–white light but no flame.

combustion spoon: also known as a deflagrating spoon, it consists of a long metal handle with a small cup at the end. Its purpose is to allow the safe introduction of a (usually heated) substance into a gas jar filled with gas, when the reaction is likely to be vigorous. *Example:* the introduction of a heated sodium pellet into a gas jar containing chlorine.

compound: a chemical consisting of two or more elements chemically bonded together. *Example:* Calcium atoms can combine with carbon atoms and oxygen atoms to make calcium carbonate ($CaCO_3$), a compound of all three atoms.

condensation: the formation of a liquid from a gas. This is a change of state, also called a phase change.

condensation nuclei: microscopic particles of dust, salt and other materials suspended in the air, that attract water molecules. The usual result is the formation of water droplets.

condensation polymer: a polymer formed by a chain of reactions in which a water molecule is eliminated as every link of the polymer is formed. *Examples:* polyesters, proteins, nylon.

conduction: (i) the exchange of heat (heat conduction) by contact with another object, or (ii) allowing the flow of electrons (electrical conduction).

conductivity: the ability of a substance to conduct. The conductivity of a solution depends on there being suitable free ions in the solution. A conducting solution is called an electrolyte. *Example:* dilute sulphuric acid.

convection: the exchange of heat energy with the surroundings produced by the flow of a fluid due to being heated or cooled.

corrosion: the oxidation of a metal. Corrosion is often regarded as unwanted and is more generally used to refer to the *slow* decay of a metal resulting from contact with gases and liquids in the environment. *Example:* Rust is the corrosion of iron.

corrosive: causing corrosion. *Example:* Sodium hydroxide (NaOH).

covalent bond: this is the most common form of strong chemical bonding and occurs when two atoms *share* electrons. *Example:* oxygen (O_2)

cracking: breaking down complex molecules into simpler compounds, as in oil refining.

crucible: a small bowl with a lip, made of heat-resistant white glazed ceramic. It is used for heating substances using a Bunsen flame.

crude oil: a chemical mixture of petroleum liquids. Crude oil forms the raw material for an oil refinery.

crystal: a substance that has grown freely so that it can develop external faces. Compare crystalline, where the atoms are not free to form individual crystals and amorphous, where the atoms are arranged irregularly.

crystalline: a solid in which the atoms, ions or molecules are organised into an orderly pattern without distinct crystal faces. *Examples:* copper(II) sulphate, sodium chloride. Compare amorphous.

crystallisation: the process in which a solute comes out of solution slowly and forms crystals. *See:* water of crystallisation.

crystal systems: seven patterns or systems into which all crystals can be grouped: cubic, hexagonal, rhombohedral, tetragonal, orthorhombic, monoclinic and triclinic.

cubic crystal system: groupings of crystals that look like cubes.

current: an electric current is produced by a flow of electrons through a conducting solid or ions through a conducting liquid. The rate of supply of this charge is measured in amperes (A).

decay (radioactive decay): the way that a radioactive element changes into another element due to loss of mass through radiation. *Example:* uranium 238 decays with the loss of an alpha particle to form thorium 234.

decomposition: the break down of a substance (for example, by heat or with the aid of a catalyst) into simpler components. In such a chemical reaction only one substance is involved. *Example:* hydrogen peroxide ($H_2O_2(aq)$) into oxygen ($O_2(g)$) and water ($H_2O(l)$).

decrepitation: when, as part of the decomposition of a substance, cracking sounds are also produced. *Example:* heating of lead nitrate ($Pb(NO_3)_2$).

dehydration: the removal of water from a substance by heating it, placing it in a dry atmosphere or using a drying (dehydrating) reagent such as concentrated sulphuric acid.

density: the mass per unit volume (e.g. g/cc).

desalinisation: the removal of all the salts from sea water, by reverse osmosis or heating the water and collecting the distillate. It is a very energy-intensive process.

desiccant: a substance that absorbs water vapour from the air. *Example:* silica gel.

desiccator: a glass bowl and lid containing a shelf. The apparatus is designed to store materials in dry air. A desiccant is placed below the shelf and the substance to be dried is placed on the shelf. The lid makes a gas-tight joint with the bowl.

destructive distillation: the heating of a material so that it decomposes entirely to release all of its volatile components. Destructive distillation is also known as pyrolysis.

detergent: a chemical based on petroleum that removes dirt.

Devarda's alloy: zinc with a trace of copper, which acts as a catalyst for reactions with the zinc.

diaphragm: a semipermeable membrane – a kind of ultrafine mesh filter – that allows only small ions to pass through. It is used in the electrolysis of brine.

diffusion: the slow mixing of one substance with another until the two substances are evenly mixed. Mixing occurs because of differences in concentration within the mixture. Diffusion works rapidly with gases, very slowly with liquids.

diffusion combustion: the form of combustion that occurs when two gases only begin to mix during ignition. As a result the flame is hollow and yellow in colour. *Example:* a candle flame.

dilute acid: an acid whose concentration has been reduced in a large proportion of water.

disinfectant: a chemical that kills bacteria and other microorganisms.

displacement reaction: a reaction that occurs because metals differ in their reactivity. If a more reactive metal is placed in a solution of a less reactive metal compound, a reaction occurs in which the more reactive metal displaces the metal ions in the solution. *Example:* when zinc metal is introduced into a solution of copper(II) sulphate (which thus contains copper ions), zinc goes into solution as zinc ions, while copper is displaced from the solution and forced to precipitate as metallic copper.

dissociate: to break bonds apart. In the case of acids, it means to break up, forming hydrogen ions. This is an example of ionisation. Strong acids dissociate completely. Weak acids are not completely ionised, and a solution of a weak acid has a relatively low concentration of hydrogen ions.

dissolve: to break down a substance in a solution without causing a reaction.

distillation: the process of separating mixtures by condensing the vapours through cooling.

distilled water: distilled water is nearly pure water and is produced by distillation of tap water. Distilled water is used in the laboratory in preference to tap water because the distillation process removes many of the impurities in tap water that may influence the chemical reactions for which the water is used.

Dreschel bottle: a tall bottle with a special stopper, designed to allow a gas to pass through a liquid. The stopper contains both inlet and outlet tubes. One tube extends below the surface of the liquid so that the gas has to pass through the liquid before it can escape to the outlet tube.

dropper funnel: a special funnel with a tap to allow the controlled release of a liquid. Also known as a dropping funnel or tap funnel.

drying agent: *See:* dehydrating agent.

dye: a coloured substance that will stick to another substance so that both appear coloured.

effervesce: to give off bubbles of gas.

effloresce: to lose water and turn to a fine powder on exposure to the air. *Example:* Sodium carbonate on the rim of a reagent bottle stopper.

electrical conductivity: *See:* conductivity

electrical potential: the energy produced by an electrochemical cell and measured by the voltage or electromotive force (emf). *See:* potential difference, electromotive force.

electrochemical cell: a cell consisting of two electrodes and an electrolyte. It can be set up to generate an electric current (usually known as a galvanic cell, an example of which is a battery), or an electric current can be passed through it to produce a chemical reaction (in which case it is called an electrolytic cell and can be used to refine metals or for electroplating).

electrochemical series: the arrangement of substances that are either oxidising or reducing agents in order of strength as a reagent, for example, with the strong oxidising agents at the top of the list and the strong reducing agents at the bottom.

electrode: a conductor that forms one terminal of a cell.

electrolysis: an electrical–chemical process that uses an electric current to cause the break-up of a compound and the movement of metal ions in a solution. The process happens in many natural situations (as for example in rusting) and is also commonly used

in industry for purifying (refining) metals or for plating metal objects with a fine, even metal coating.

electrolyte: an ionic solution that conducts electricity.

electrolytic cell: *See:* electrochemical cell.

electromotive force (emf): the force set up in an electric circuit by a potential difference.

electron: a tiny, negatively charged particle that is part of an atom. The flow of electrons through a solid material such as a wire produces an electric current.

electron configuration: the pattern in which electrons are arranged in shells around the nucleus of an atom. *Example:* chlorine has the configuration 2, 8, 7.

electroplating: depositing a thin layer of a metal on to the surface of another substance using electrolysis.

element: a substance that cannot be decomposed into simpler substance by chemical means. *Examples:* calcium, iron, gold.

emulsion: tiny droplets of one substance dispersed in another. One common oil in water emulsion is called milk. Because the tiny droplets tend to come together, another stabilising substance is often needed. Soaps and detergents are such agents, wrapping the particles of grease and oil in a stable coat. Photographic film is an example of a solid emulsion.

endothermic reaction: a reaction that takes in heat. *Example:* when ammonium chloride is dissolved in water.

end point: the stage in a titration when the reaction between the titrant (added from a burette) and the titrate (in the flask) is complete. The end point is normally recognised by use of an indicator which has been added to

the titrate. In an acid–base reaction this is also called the neutralisation point.

enzyme: biological catalysts in the form of proteins in the body that speed up chemical reactions. Every living cell contains hundreds of enzymes that help the processes of life continue.

ester: organic compounds formed by the reaction of an alcohol with an acid and which often have a fruity taste. *Example:* ethyl acetate ($CH_3COOC_2H_5$).

evaporation: the change of state of a liquid to a gas. Evaporation happens below the boiling point and is used as a method of separating the materials in a solution.

excess, to: if a reactant has been added to another reactant in excess, it has exceeded the amount required to complete the reaction.

exothermic reaction: a reaction that gives out substantial amounts of heat. *Example:* sucrose and concentrated sulphuric acid.

explosive: a substance which, when a shock is applied to it, decomposes very rapidly, releasing a very large amount of heat and creating a large volume of gases as a shock wave.

fats: semisolid, energy-rich compounds derived from plants or animals, made of carbon, hydrogen and oxygen. These are examples of esters.

ferment: to break down a substance by microorganisms in the absence of oxygen. *Example:* fermentation of sugar to ethanol during the production of alcoholic drinks.

filtrate: the liquid that has passed through a filter.

filtration: the separation of a liquid from a solid using a membrane with small holes (i.e. a filter paper).

flame: a mixture of gases undergoing burning. A solid or liquid must produce a gas before it can react with oxygen and burn with a flame.

flammable (also inflammable): able to burn (in air). *Opposite:* non-flammable.

flocculation: the grouping together of small particles in a suspension to form particles large enough to settle out as a precipitate. Flocculation is usually caused by the presence of a flocculating agent. *Example:* calcium ions are the flocculating agent for suspended clay particles.

fluid: able to flow; either a liquid or a gas.

fluorescent: a substance that gives out visible light when struck by invisible waves, such as ultraviolet rays.

flux: a material used to make it easier for a liquid to flow. A flux dissolves metal oxides and so prevents a metal from oxidising while being heated.

foam: a substance that is sufficiently gelatinous to be able to contain bubbles of gas. The gas bulks up the substance, making it behave as though it were semirigid.

fossil fuels: hydrocarbon compounds that have been formed from buried plant and animal remains. High pressures and temperatures lasting over millions of years are required. *Examples:* The fossil fuels are coal, oil and natural gas.

fraction: a group of similar components of a mixture. *Example:* In the petroleum industry the light fractions of crude oil are those with the smallest molecules, while the medium and heavy fractions have larger molecules.

fractional distillation: the separation of the components of a liquid mixture by heating them to their boiling points.

fractionating column: a glass column designed to allow different fractions to be separated when they boil. In industry, it may be called a fractionating tower.

free radical: a very reactive atom or group with a 'spare' electron. *Example:* methyl, $CH_3\bullet$.

freezing point: the temperature at which a substance undergoes a phase change from a liquid to a solid. It is the same temperature as the melting point.

fuel: a concentrated form of chemical energy. The main sources of fuels (called fossil fuels because they were formed by geological processes) are coal, crude oil and natural gas.

fuel rods: the rods of uranium or other radioactive material used as a fuel in nuclear power stations.

fume chamber or fume cupboard: a special laboratory chamber fitted with a protective glass shield and containing a powerful extraction fan to remove toxic fumes.

fuming: an unstable liquid that gives off a gas. Very concentrated acid solutions are often fuming solutions. *Example:* fuming nitric acid.

galvanising: applying a thin zinc coating to protect another metal.

gamma rays: waves of radiation produced as the nucleus of a radioactive element rearranges itself into a tighter cluster of protons and neutrons. Gamma rays carry enough energy to damage living cells.

gangue: the unwanted material in an ore.

gas/gaseous phase: a form of matter in which the molecules form no definite shape and are free to move about to uniformly fill any vessel they are put in. A gas can easily be compressed into a much smaller volume.

gas syringe: a glass syringe with a graduated cylinder designed to collect and measure small amounts of gases produced during an experiment.

gelatinous precipitate: a precipitate that has a jelly-like appearance. *Example:* iron (III) hydroxide. Because a gelatinous precipitate is mostly water, it is of a similar density to water and will float or lie suspended in the liquid. *See:* granular precipitate.

glass: a transparent silicate without any crystal growth. It has a glassy lustre and breaks with a curved fracture. Note that some minerals have all these features and are therefore natural glasses. Household glass is a synthetic silicate.

glucose: the most common of the natural sugars ($C_6H_{12}O_6$). It occurs as the polymer known as cellulose, the fibre in plants. Starch is also a form of glucose.

granular precipitate: a precipitate that has a grain-like appearance. *Example:* lead(II) hydroxide. *See:* gelatinous precipitate.

gravimetric analysis: a quantitative form of analysis in which the mass (weight) of the reactants and products is measured.

group: a vertical column in the Periodic Table. There are eight groups in the table. Their numbers correspond to the number of electrons in the outer shell of the atoms in the group. *Example:* Group 1: member, sodium.

Greenhouse Effect: an increase in the global air temperature as a result of heat released from burning fossil fuels being absorbed by carbon dioxide in the atmosphere.

Greenhouse gas: any of various the gases that contribute to the Greenhouse Effect. *Example:* carbon dioxide.

half-life: the time it takes for the radiation coming from a sample of a radioactive element to decrease by half.

halide: a salt of one of the halogens.

halogen: one of a group of elements including chlorine, bromine, iodine and fluorine in Group 7 of the Periodic Table.

heat: the energy that is transferred when a substance is at a different temperature to that of its surroundings. *See:* endothermic and exothermic reactions.

heat capacity: the ratio of the heat supplied to a substance, compared with the rise in temperature that is produced.

heat of combustion: the amount of heat given off by a mole of a substance during combustion. This heat is a property of the substance and is the same no matter what kind of combustion is involved. *Example:* heat of combustion of carbon is 94.05 kcal ($\times$ 4.18 = 393.1 kJ).

hydrate: a solid compound in crystalline form that contains water molecules. Hydrates commonly form when a solution of a soluble salt is evaporated. The water that forms part of a hydrate crystal is known as the 'water of crystallisation'. It can usually be removed by heating, leaving an anhydrous salt.

hydration: the process of absorption of water by a substance. In some cases hydration makes the substance change colour; in many other cases there is no colour change, simply a change in volume. *Example:* dark blue hydrated copper(II) sulphate ($CuSO_4 \bullet 5H_2O$) can be heated to produce white anhydrous copper(II) sulphate ($CuSO_4$).

hydride: a compound containing just hydrogen and another element, most often a metal.

Examples: water (H_2O), methane (CH_4) and phosphine (PH_3).

hydrous: hydrated with water. *See:* anhydrous.

hydrocarbon: a compound in which only hydrogen and carbon atoms are present. Most fuels are hydrocarbons, as is the simple plastic, polyethene. *Example:* methane CH_4.

hydrogen bond: a type of attractive force that holds one molecule to another. It is one of the weaker forms of intermolecular attractive force. *Example:* hydrogen bonds occur in water.

ignition temperature: the temperature at which a substance begins to burn.

immiscible: will not mix with another substance. e.g., oil and water.

incandescent: glowing or shining with heat. *Example:* tungsten filament in an incandescent light bulb.

incomplete combustion: combustion in which only some of the reactant or reactants combust, or the products are not those that would be obtained if all the reactions went to completion. It is uncommon for combustion to be complete and incomplete combustion is more frequent. *Example:* incomplete combustion of carbon in oxygen produces carbon monoxide and not carbon dioxide.

indicator (acid–base indicator): a substance or mixture of substances used to test the acidity or alkalinity of a substance. An indicator changes colour depending on the acidity of the solution being tested. Many indicators are complicated organic substances. Some indicators used in the laboratory include Universal Indicator, litmus, phenolphthalein, methyl orange and bromothymol. *See:* Universal Indicator.

induction period: the time taken for a reaction to reach ignition temperature. During this period, no apparent reaction occurs, then the materials appear to undergo spontaneous combustion.

inert: unreactive.

inhibitor: a substance that prevents a reaction from occurring.

inorganic substance: a substance that does not contain carbon and hydrogen. *Examples:* NaCl, $CaCO_3$.

insoluble: a substance that will not dissolve.

ion: an atom, or group of atoms, that has gained or lost one or more electrons and so developed an electrical charge. Ions behave differently from electrically neutral atoms and molecules. They can move in an electric field, and they can also bind strongly to solvent molecules such as water. Positively charged ions are called cations; negatively charged ions are called anions. Ions can carry an electrical current through solutions.

ionic bond: the form of bonding that occurs between two ions when the ions have opposite charges. *Example:* sodium cations bond with chloride anions to form common salt (NaCl) when a salty solution is evaporated. Ionic bonds are strong bonds except in the presence of a solvent. *See:* bond.

ionic compound: a compound that consists of ions. *Example:* NaCl.

ionise: to break up neutral molecules into oppositely charged ions or to convert atoms into ions by the loss of electrons.

ionisation: a process that creates ions.

isotope: an atom that has the same number of protons in its nucleus, but which has a different mass. *Example:* carbon 12 and carbon 14.

Kipp's apparatus: a piece of glassware consisting of three

chambers, designed to provide a continuous and regulated production of gas by bringing the reactants into contact in a controlled way.

lanthanide series or lanthanide metals: a series of 15 similar metallic elements between lanthanum and lutetium. They are transition metals and also also called rare earths.

latent heat: the amount of heat that is absorbed or released during the process of changing state between gas, liquid or solid. For example, heat is absorbed when a substance melts and it is released again when the substance solidifies.

lattice: a regular arrangement of atoms, ions or molecules in a crystalline solid.

leaching: the extraction of a substance by percolating a solvent through a material. *Example:* when water flows through an ore, some of the heavy metals in it may be leached out causing environmental pollution.

Liebig condenser: a piece of glassware consisting of a sloping water-cooled tube. The design allows a volatile material to be condensed and collected.

liquefaction: to make something liquid.

liquid/liquid phase: a form of matter that has a fixed volume but no fixed shape.

lime (quicklime): calcium oxide (CaO). A white, caustic solid, manufactured by heating limestone and used for making mortar, fertiliser or bleach.

limewater: an aqueous solution of calcium hydroxide, used especially to detect the presence of carbon dioxide.

litmus: an indicator obtained from lichens. Used as a solution or impregnated into paper (litmus paper), which is dampened before use. Litmus turns red under acid conditions and purple in alkaline conditions. Litmus is a crude indicator when compared with Universal Indicator.

load (electronics): an impedance or circuit that receives or develops the output of a cell or other power supply.

lustre: the shininess of a substance.

malleable: able to be pressed or hammered into shape.

manometer: a device for measuring gas pressure. A simple manometer is made by partly filling a U-shaped rubber tube with water and connecting one end to the source of gas whose pressure is to be measured. The pressure is always relative to atmospheric pressure.

mass: the amount of matter in an object. In everyday use the word weight is often used (somewhat incorrectly) to mean mass.

matter: anything that has mass and takes up space.

melting point: the temperature at which a substance changes state from a solid phase to a liquid phase. It is the same as freezing point.

membrane: a thin, flexible sheet. A semipermeable membrane has microscopic holes of a size that will selectively allow some ions and molecules to pass through but hold others back. It thus acts as a kind of filter. *Example:* a membrane used for osmosis.

meniscus: the curved surface of a liquid that forms in a small bore or capillary tube. The meniscus is convex (bulges upwards) for mercury and is concave (sags downwards) for water.

metal: a class of elements that is a good conductor of electricity and heat, has a metallic lustre, is malleable and ductile, forms cations and has oxides that are bases. Metals are formed as cations held together by a sea of electrons. A metal may also be an alloy of these elements. *Example:* sodium, calcium, gold. *See:* alloy, metalloid, non-metal.

metallic bonding: cations reside in a 'sea' of mobile electrons. It allows metals to be good conductors and means that they are not brittle. *See:* bonding.

metallic lustre: *See:* lustre.

metalloid: a class of elements intermediate in properties between metals and non-metals. Metalloids are also called semi-metals or semiconductors. *Example:* silicon, germanium, antimony. *See:* metal, non-metal, semiconductor.

micronutrient: an element that the body requires in small amounts. Another term is trace element.

mineral: a solid substance made of just one element or compound. *Example:* calcite is a mineral because it consists only of calcium carbonate; halite is a mineral because it contains only sodium chloride.

mineral acid: an acid that does not contain carbon and which attacks minerals. Hydrochloric, sulphuric and nitric acids are the main mineral acids.

miscible: capable of being mixed.

mixing combustion: the form of combustion that occurs when two gases thoroughly mix before they ignite and so produce almost complete combustion. *Example:* when a Bunsen flame is blue.

mixture: a material that can be separated into two or more substances using physical means. *Example:* a mixture of copper(II) sulphate and cadmium sulphide can be separated by filtration.

molar mass: the mass per mole of atoms of an element. It has the same value and uses the same units as atomic weight. *Example:* molar mass of chlorine is 35.45 g/mol. *See:* atomic weight.

mole: 1 mole is the amount of a substance which contains Avagadro's number (6×10^{23}) of particles. *Example:* 1 mole of carbon-12 weighs exactly 12 g.

molecular mass: *See:* molar mass.

molecular weight: *See:* molar mass.

molecule: a group of two or more atoms held together by chemical bonds. *Example:* O_2.

monoclinic system: a grouping of crystals that look like double-ended chisel blades.

monomer: a small molecule and building block for larger chain molecules or polymers ('mono' means one, 'mer' means part). *Examples:* tetrafluoroethene for teflon, ethene for polyethene.

native element: an element that occurs in an uncombined state. *Examples:* sulphur, gold.

native metal: a pure form of a metal, not combined as a compound. Native metal is more common in poorly reactive elements than in those that are very reactive. *Examples:* copper, gold.

net ionic reaction: the overall, or net, change that occurs in a reaction, seen in terms of ions.

neutralisation: the reaction of acids and bases to produce a salt and water. The reaction causes hydrogen from the acid and hydroxide from the base to be changed to water. *Example:* hydrochloric acid reacts with, and neutralises, sodium hydroxide to form the salt sodium chloride (common salt) and water. The term is more generally used for any reaction in which the pH changes toward 7.0, which is the pH of a neutral solution. *See:* pH.

neutralisation point: *See:* end point.

neutron: a particle inside the nucleus of an atom that is neutral and has no charge.

newton (N): the unit of force required to give one kilogram an acceleration of one metre per second every second (1 ms^{-2}).

nitrate: a compound that includes nitrogen and oxygen and contains more oxygen than a nitrite. Nitrate ions have the chemical formula NO_3^-. *Examples:* sodium nitrate $NaNO_3$ and lead nitrate $Pb(NO_3)_2$.

nitrite: a compound that includes nitrogen and oxygen and contains less oxygen than a nitrate. Nitrite ions have the chemical formula NO_2^-. *Example:* sodium nitrite $NaNO_2$.

noble gases: the members of Group 8 of the Periodic Table: helium, neon, argon, krypton, xenon, radon. These gases are almost entirely unreactive.

noble metals: silver, gold, platinum and mercury. These are the least reactive metals.

non-combustible: a substance that will not combust or burn. *Example:* carbon dioxide.

non-metal: a brittle substance that does not conduct electricity. *Examples:* sulphur, phosphorus, all gases. *See:* metal, metalloid.

normal salt: salts that do not contain a hydroxide (OH^-) ion, which would make them basic salts, or a hydrogen ion, which would make them acid salts. *Example:* sodium chloride (NaCl).

nucleus: the small, positively charged particle at the centre of an atom. The nucleus is responsible for most of the mass of an atom.

opaque: a substance that will not transmit light so that it is impossible to see through it. Most solids are opaque.

ore: a rock containing enough of a useful substance to make mining it worthwhile. *Example:* bauxite, aluminium ore.

organic acid: an acid containing carbon and hydrogen. *Example:* methanoic (formic) acid (HCOOH).

organic chemistry: the study of organic compounds.

organic compound (organic substance; organic material): a compound (or substance) that contains carbon and usually hydrogen. (The carbonates are usually excluded.) *Examples:* methane (CH_4), chloromethane (CH_3Cl), ethene (C_2H_4), ethanol (C_2H_5OH), ethanoic acid (C_2H_3OOH), etc.

organic solvent: an organic substance that will dissolve other substances. *Example:* carbon tetrachloride (CCl_4).

osmosis: a process whereby molecules of a liquid solvent move through a semipermeable membrane from a region of low concentration of a solute to a region with a high concentration of a solute.

oxidation–reduction reaction (redox reaction): reaction in which oxidation and reduction occurs; a reaction in which electrons are transferred. *Example:* copper and oxygen react to produce copper(II) oxide. The copper is oxidised, and oxygen is reduced.

oxidation: combination with oxygen or a reaction in which an atom, ion or molecule loses electrons to an oxidising agent. (Note that an oxidising agent does not have to contain oxygen.) The opposite of oxidation is reduction. *See:* reduction.

oxidation number (oxidation state): the effective charge on an atom in a compound. An increase in oxidation number corresponds to oxidation, and a decrease to reduction. Shown in Roman numerals. *Example:* manganate(IV).

oxidation state: *See:* oxidation number.

oxide: a compound that includes oxygen and one other element. *Example:* copper oxide (CuO).

oxidise: to combine with or gain oxygen or to react such that an atom, ion or molecule loses electrons to an oxidising agent.

oxidising agent: a substance that removes electrons from another substance being oxidised (and therefore is itself reduced) in a redox reaction. *Example:* chlorine (Cl_2).

ozone: a form of oxygen whose molecules contain three atoms of oxygen. Ozone is regarded as a beneficial gas when high in the atmosphere because it blocks ultraviolet rays. It is a harmful gas when breathed in, so low level ozone which is produced as part of city smog is regarded as a form of pollution. The ozone layer is the uppermost part of the stratosphere.

partial pressure: the pressure a gas in a mixture would exert if it alone occupied a flask. *Example:* oxygen makes up about a fifth of the atmosphere. Its partial pressure is therefore about a fifth of normal atmospheric pressure.

pascal: the unit of pressure, equal to one newton per square metre of surface. *See:* newton.

patina: a surface coating that develops on metals and protects them from further corrosion. *Example:* the green coating of copper carbonate that forms on copper statues.

percolate: to move slowly through the pores of a rock.

period: a row in the Periodic Table.

Periodic Table: a chart organising elements by atomic number and chemical properties into groups and periods.

pestle and mortar: a pestle is a ceramic rod with a rounded end, a mortar is a ceramic dish. Pestle and mortar are used together to pound or grind solids into fine powders.

Petri dish: a shallow glass or plastic dish with a lid.

petroleum: a natural mixture of a range of gases, liquids and solids derived from the decomposed remains of plants and animals.

pH: a measure of the hydrogen ion concentration in a liquid. Neutral is pH 7.0; numbers greater than this are alkaline; smaller numbers are acidic. *See:* neutralisation, acid, base.

pH meter: a device that accurately measures the pH of a solution. A pH meter is a voltmeter that measures the electric potential difference between two electrodes (which are attached to the meter through a probe) when they are submerged in a solution. The readings are shown on a dial or digital display.

phase: a particular state of matter. A substance may exist as a solid, liquid or gas and may change between these phases with addition or removal of energy. *Examples:* ice, liquid and vapour are the three phases of water. Ice undergoes a phase change to water when heat energy is added.

phosphor: any material that glows when energised by ultraviolet or electron beams, such as in fluorescent tubes and cathode ray tubes. Phosphors, such as phosphorus, emit light after the source of excitation is cut off. This is why they glow in the dark. By contrast, fluorescers, such as fluorite, only emit light while they are being excited by ultraviolet light or an electron beam.

photochemical smog: photochemical reactions are caused by the energy of sunlight. Photochemical smog is a mixture of tiny particles and a brown haze caused by the reaction of colourless nitric oxide from vehicle exhausts and oxygen of the air to form brown nitrogen dioxide.

photon: a parcel of light energy.

photosynthesis: the process by which plants use the energy of the Sun to make the compounds they need for life. In photosynthesis, six molecules of carbon dioxide from the air combine with six molecules of water, forming one molecule of glucose (sugar) and releasing six molecules of oxygen back into the atmosphere.

pipe-clay triangle: a device made from three small pieces of ceramic tube which are wired together in the shape of a triangle. Pipe-clay triangles are used to support round-bottomed dishes when they are heated in a Bunsen flame.

pipette: a log, slender, glass tube used, in conjunction with a pipette filler, to draw up and then transfer accurately measured amounts of liquid.

plastic: (material) a carbon-based substance consisting of long chains (polymers) of simple molecules. The word plastic is commonly restricted to synthetic polymers. *Examples:* polyvinyl chloride, nylon: **(property)** a material is plastic if it can be made to change shape easily. Plastic materials will remain in the new shape. (Compare with elastic, a property whereby a material goes back to its original shape.)

pneumatic trough: a shallow water-filled glass dish used to house a beehive shelf and a gas jar as part of the apparatus for collecting a gas over water.

polar solvent: a solvent in which the atoms have partial electric charges. *Example:* water.

polymer: a compound that is made of long chains by combining molecules (called monomers) as repeating units. ('Poly' means many, 'mer' means part.) *Examples:* polytetrafluoroethene or Teflon from tetrafluoroethene, Terylene from terephthalic acid and ethane-1,2-diol (ethylene glycol).

polymerisation: a chemical reaction in which large numbers of similar molecules arrange themselves into large molecules, usually long chains. This process usually happens when there is a suitable catalyst present. *Example:* ethene gas reacts to form polyethene in the presence of certain catalysts.

polymorphism: (meaning many shapes) the tendency of some materials to have more than one solid form. *Example:* carbon as diamond, graphite and buckminsterfullerene.

porous: a material containing many small holes or cracks. Quite often the pores are connected, and liquids, such as water or oil, can move through them.

potential difference: a measure of the work that must be done to move an electric charge from one point to the other in a circuit. Potential difference is measured in volts, V. *See:* electrical potential.

precious metal: silver, gold, platinum, iridium and palladium. Each is prized for its rarity.

precipitate: a solid substance formed as a result of a chemical reaction between two liquids or gases. *Example:* iron(III) hydroxide is precipitated when sodium hydroxide solution is added to iron(III) chloride. *See:* gelatinous precipitate, granular precipitate.

preservative: a substance that prevents the natural organic decay processes from occurring. Many substances can be used safely for this purpose, including sulphites and nitrogen gas.

pressure: the force per unit area measured in pascals. *See:* pascal, atmospheric pressure.

product: a substance produced by a chemical reaction. *Example:* when the reactants copper and oxygen react, they produce the product, copper oxide.

proton: a positively charged particle in the nucleus of an atom that balances out the charge of the surrounding electrons.

proton number: this is the modern expression for atomic number. *See:* atomic number.

purify: to remove all impurities from a mixture, perhaps by precipitation, or filtration.

pyrolysis: chemical decomposition brought about by heat. *Example:* decomposition of lead nitrate. *See:* destructive distillation.

pyrometallurgy: refining a metal from its ore using heat. A blast furnace or smelter is the main equipment used.

quantitative: measurement of the amounts of constituents of a substance, for example by mass or volume. *See:* gravimetric analysis, volumetric analysis.

radiation: the exchange of energy with the surroundings through the transmission of waves or particles of energy. Radiation is a form of energy transfer that can happen through space; no intervening medium is required (as would be the case for conduction and convection).

radical: an atom, molecule, or ion with at least one unpaired electron. *Example:* nitrogen monoxide (NO).

radioactive: emitting radiation or particles from the nucleus of its atoms.

radioactive decay: a change in a radioactive element due to loss of mass through radiation. For example, uranium decays (changes) to lead.

reactant: a starting material that takes part in, and undergoes, change during a chemical reaction. *Example:* hydrochloric acid and calcium carbonate are reactants; the reaction produces the products calcium chloride, carbon dioxide and water.

reaction: the recombination of two substances using parts of each substance to produce new substances. *Example:* the reactants sodium chloride and sulphuric acid react and recombine to form the products sodium sulphate, chlorine and water.

reactivity: the tendency of a substance to react with other substances. The term is most widely used in comparing the reactivity of metals. Metals are arranged in a reactivity series.

reactivity series: the series of metals organised in order of their reactivity, with the most reactive metals, such as sodium, at the top and the least react metals, such as gold, at the bottom. Hydrogen is usually included in the series for comparative purposes.

reagent: a commonly available substance (reactant) used to create a reaction. Reagents are the chemicals normally kept on chemistry laboratory benches. Many substances called reagents are most commonly used for test purposes.

redox reaction (oxidation–reduction reaction): a reaction that involves oxidation and reduction; a reactions in which electrons are transferred. *See:* oxidation–reduction.

reducing agent: a substance that gives electrons to another substance being reduced (and therefore itself being oxidised) in a redox reaction. *Example:* hydrogen sulphide (H_2S).

reduction: the removal of oxygen from, or the addition of hydrogen to, a compound. Also a reaction in which an atom, ion or molecule gains electrons from an reducing agent. (The opposite of reduction is oxidation.)

reduction tube: a boiling tube with a small hole near the closed end. The tube is mounted horizontally, a sample is placed in the tube and a reducing gas, such as carbon monoxide, is passed through the tube. The oxidised gas escapes through the small hole.

refining: separating a mixture into the simpler substances of which it is made.

reflux distillation system: a form of distillation using a Liebig condenser placed vertically, so that all the vapours created during boiling are condensed back into the liquid, rather than escaping. In this way, the concentration of all the reactants remains constant.

relative atomic mass: in the past a measure of the mass of an atom on a scale relative to the mass of an atom of hydrogen, where hydrogen is 1. Nowadays a measure of the mass of an atom relative to the mass of one twelfth of an atom of carbon-12. If the relative atomic mass is given as a rounded figure, it is called an approximate relative atomic mass. *Examples*: chlorine 35, calcium 40, gold 197. *See:* atomic mass, atomic weight.

reversible reaction: a reaction in which the products can be transformed back into their original chemical form. *Example:* heated iron reacts with steam to produce iron oxide and hydrogen. If the hydrogen is passed over this heated oxide, it forms iron and steam. $3Fe + 4H_2O \rightleftharpoons Fe_3O_4 + 4H_2$.

roast: heating a substance for a long time at a high temperature, as in a furnace.

rust: the product of the corrosion of iron and steel in the presence of air and water.

salt: a compound, often involving a metal, that is the reaction product of an acid and a base, or of two elements. (Note 'salt' is also the common word for sodium chloride, common salt or table salt.) *Example:* sodium chloride (NaCl) and potassium sulphate (K_2SO_4) *See:* acid salt, basic salt, normal salt.

salt bridge: a permeable material soaked in a salt solution that allows ions to be transferred from one container to another. The salt solution remains unchanged during this transfer. *Example:* sodium sulphate used as a salt bridge in a galvanic cell.

saponification: a reaction between a fat and a base that produces a soap.

saturated: a state in which a liquid can hold no more of a substance. If any more of the substance is added, it will not dissolve.

saturated hydrocarbon: a hydrocarbon in which the carbon atoms are held with single bonds. *Example:* ethane (C_2H_6).

saturated solution: a solution that holds the maximum possible amount of dissolved material. When saturated, the rate of dissolving solid and that of recrystallisation solid are the same, and a condition of equilibrium is reached. The amount of material in solution varies with the temperature; cold solutions can hold less dissolved solid material than hot solutions. Gases are more soluble in cold liquids than in hot liquids.

sediment: material that settles out at the bottom of a liquid when it is still. A precipitate is one form of sediment.

semiconductor: a material of intermediate conductivity. Semiconductor devices often use silicon when they are made as part of diodes, transistors or integrated circuits. Elements intermediate between metals and non-metals are also sometimes called semiconductors. *Example:* germanium oxide, germanium. *See:* metalloid.

semipermeable membrane: a thin material that acts as a fine sieve or filter, allowing small molecules to pass, but holding large molecules back.

separating column: used in chromatography. A tall glass tube containing a porous disc near the base and filled with a substance (for example, aluminium oxide, which is known as a stationary phase) that can adsorb materials on its surface. When a mixture is passed through the column, fractions are retarded by differing amounts, so that each fraction is washed through the column in sequence.

separating funnel: a pear-shaped, glassware funnel designed to permit the separation of immiscible liquids by simply pouring off the more dense liquid while leaving the less dense liquid in the funnel.

series circuit: an electrical circuit in which all of the components are joined end to end in a line.

shell: the term used to describe the imaginary ball-shaped surface outside the nucleus of an atom that would be formed by a set of electrons of similar energy. The outermost shell is known as the valence shell. *Example:* neon has shells containing 2 and 8 electrons.

side-arm boiling tube: a boiling tube with an integral glass pipe near its open end. The side arm is normally used for the entry or exit of a gas.

simple distillation: the distillation of a substance when only one volatile fraction is to be collected. Simple distillation uses a Liebig condenser arranged almost horizontally. When the liquid mixture is heated and vapours are produced, they enter the condenser and then flow away from the flask and can be collected. *Example:* simple distillation of ethanoic acid.

slag: a mixture of substances that are waste products of a furnace. Most slags are composed mainly of silicates.

smelting: roasting a substance in order to extract the metal contained in it.

smog: a mixture of smoke and fog. The term is used to describe city fogs in which there is a large proportion of particulate matter (tiny pieces of carbon from exhausts) and also a high concentration of sulphur and nitrogen gases and probably ozone. *See:* photochemical smog.

smokeless fuel: a fuel which has been subjected to partial pyrolysis, such that there is no more loose particulate matter remaining. *Example:* Coke is a smokeless fuel.

solid/solid phase: a rigid form of matter which maintains its shape, whatever its container.

solubility: the maximum amount of a substance that can be contained in a solvent.

soluble: readily dissolvable in a solvent.

solute: a substance that has dissolved. *Example:* sodium chloride in water.

solution: a mixture of a liquid (the solvent) and at least one other substance of lesser abundance (the solute). Mixtures can be separated by physical means, for example, by evaporation and cooling. *See:* aqueous solution.

solvent: the main substance in a solution.

spectator ions: the ionic part of a compound that does not play an active part in a reaction. *Example:* when magnesium ribbon is placed in copper(II) sulphate solution, the copper is displaced from the solution by the magnesium, while the sulphate ion (SO_4^{2-}) plays no part in the reaction and so behaves as a spectator ion.

spectrum: a progressive series arranged using a characteristic etc. *Examples:* the range of colours that make up visible light (as seen in a rainbow) or across all electromagnetic radiation, arranged in progression according to their wavelength.

spontaneous combustion: the effect of a very reactive material or combination of reactants that suddenly reach their ignition temperature and begin to combust rapidly.

standard temperature and pressure (STP): 0°C at one atmosphere (a pressure which supports a column of mercury 760 mm high). Also given as 0°C at 100 kilopascals. *See:* atmospheric pressure.

state of matter: the physical form of matter. There are three states of matter: liquid, solid and gaseous.

stationary phase: a name given to a material which is used as a medium for separating a liquid mixture in chromatography.

strong acid: an acid that has completely dissociated (ionised) in water. Mineral acids are strong acids.

sublime/sublimation: the change of a substance from solid to gas, or vice versa, without going through a liquid phase. *Example:* iodine sublimes from a purple solid to a purple gas.

substance: a type of material, including mixtures.

sulphate: a compound that includes sulphur and oxygen and contains more oxygen than a sulphite. Sulphate ions have the chemical formula SO_4^{2-}. *Examples:* calcium sulphate $CaSO_4$ (the main constituent of gypsum) and aluminium sulphate $Al_2(SO_4)_3$ (an alum).

sulphide: a sulphur compound that contains no oxygen. Sulphide ions have the chemical formula S^{2-}. *Example:* hydrogen sulphide (H_2S).

sulphite: a compound that includes sulphur and oxygen but contains less oxygen than a sulphate. Sulphite ions have the chemical formula SO_3^{2-}. *Example:* sodium sulphite Na_2SO_3.

supercooling: the ability of some substances to cool below their normal freezing point. *Example:* sodium thiosulphate.

supersaturated solution: a solution in which the amount of solute is greater than that which would normally be expected in a saturated solution. Most solids are more soluble in hot solutions than in cold. If a hot saturated solution is made up, the solution can be rapidly cooled down below its freezing point before it begins to solidify. This is a supersaturated solution.

surface tension: the force that operates on the surface of a liquid and which makes it act as though it were covered with an invisible, elastic film.

suspension: a mist of tiny particles in a liquid.

synthesis: a reaction in which a substance is formed from simpler reactants. *Example:* hydrogen gas and chlorine gas react to sythesise hydrogen chloride gas. The term can also be applied to polymerisation of organic compounds.

synthetic: does not occur naturally but has to be manufactured. Commonly used in the name 'synthetic fibre'.

tare: an allowance made for the weight of a container.

tarnish: a coating that develops as a result of the reaction between a metal and substances in the air. The most common form of tarnishing is a very thin, transparent oxide coating.

terminal: one of the electrodes of a battery.

test (chemical): a reagent or a procedure used to reveal the presence of another reagent. *Example:* litmus and other indicators are used to test the acidity or alkalinity of a substance.

test tube: A thin, glass tube, closed at one end and used for chemical tests, etc. The composition and thickness of the glass is such that, while it is inert to most chemical reactions, it may not sustain very high temperatures but can usually be heated in a Bunsen flame. *See:* boiling tube.

thermal decomposition: the breakdown of a substance using heat. *See* pyrolysis.

thermoplastic: a plastic that will soften and can be moulded repeatedly into shape on heating and will set into the moulded shape as it cools.

thermoset: a plastic that will set into a moulded shape as it cools, but which cannot be made soft by reheating.

thistle funnel: a narrow tube, expanded at the top into a thistlehead-shaped vessel. It is used as a funnel when introducing small amounts of liquid reactant. When fitted with a tap, it can be used to control the rate of entry of a reactant. *See:* burette.

titration: the analysis of the composition of a substance in a solution by measuring the volume of that solution (the titrant, normally in a burette) needed to react with a given volume of another solution (the titrate, normally placed in a flask). An indicator is often used to signal change. *Example:* neutralisation of sodium hydroxide using hydrochloric acid in an acid–base titration. *See:* end point.

toxic: poisonous.

transition metals: the group of metals that belong to the d-block of the Periodic Table. Transition metals commonly have a number of differently coloured oxidation states. *Examples:* iron, vanadium.

Universal Indicator: a mixture of indicators commonly used in the laboratory because of its reliability. Used as a solution or impregnated into paper (Indicator paper), which is dampened before use. Universal Indicator changes colour from purple in a strongly alkaline solution through green when the solution is neutral to red in strongly acidic solutions. Universal Indicator is more accurate than litmus paper but less accurate than a pH meter.

unsaturated hydrocarbon: a hydrocarbon, in which at least one bond is a double or triple bond. Hydrogen atoms can be added to unsaturated compounds to form saturated compounds. *Example:* ethene, C_2H_4 or $CH_2=CH_2$.

vacuum: a container from which air has been removed using a pump.

valency: the number of bonds that an atom can form. *Examples:* calcium has a valency of 2 and bromine a valency of 1

valency shell: the outermost shell of an atom. *See:* shell.

vapour: the gaseous phase of a substance that is a liquid or a solid at that temperature. *Examples:* water vapour is the gaseous form of water, iodine vapour is the gaseous form of solid iodine. *See:* gas.

vein: a fissure in rock that has filled with ore or other mineral-bearing rock.

viscous: slow-moving, syrupy. A liquid that has a low viscosity is said to be mobile.

volatile: readily forms a gas.

volatile fraction: the part of a liquid mixture that will vaporise readily under the conditions prevailing during the reaction. *See:* fraction, vapour.

water of crystallisation: the water molecules absorbed into the crystalline structure as a liquid changes to a solid. *Example:* hydrated copper(II) sulphate $CuSO_4•5H_2O$. *See:* hydrate.

weak acid and **weak base**: an acid or base that has only partly dissociated (ionised) in water. Most organic acids are weak acids. *See:* organic acid.

weight: the gravitational force on a substance. *See:* mass.

X-rays: a form of very short wave radiation.

MASTER INDEX

USING THIS MASTER INDEX

Here are the 12 volumes in the *ChemLab* set.

Volume
Number   *Title*

1:   Gases, Liquids and Solids
2:   Elements, Compounds and Mixtures
3:   The Periodic Table
4:   Metals
5:   Acids, Bases and Salts
6:   Heat and Combustion
7:   Oxidation and Reduction
8:   Air and Water Chemistry
9:   Carbon Chemistry
10: Energy and Chemical Change
11: Preparations
12: Tests

An example index entry:

Index entries are
listed alphabetically

platinum **2:**6, 7; **3:**10, 28, 29; **4:**7, 8

The volume number is shown in bold for each entry. In this case the index entry platinum is found in three titles: Elements, Mixtures and Compounds, The Periodic Table and Metals.

The page references in each volume. In this case: pages 6 and 7 of the title Elements, Mixtures and Compounds; pages 10, 28 and 29 of the title The Periodic Table and pages 7 and 8 of the title Metals.